# IN PLAIN SIGHT

OBSESSIONS, MORALS & DOMESTIC LAUGHTER

Other Books by Michael Anania

# IN PLAIN SIGHT

OBSESSIONS, MORALS & DOMESTIC LAUGHTER

## MICHAEL ANANIA

ASPHODEL PRESS

MOYER BELL LIMITED

MOUNT KISCO, NEW YORK & LONDON

For Elliott Anderson, Caroline Rand Herron, Kathleen Maloney, and Christine Newman with gratitude.

Published by Asphodel Press

Some of these pieces were first published in *Chicago* Magazine, *The Chicago Tribune, Partisan Review* and *StoryQuarterley*.

**First Edition**

**LIBRARY OF CONGRESS**

**CATALOGING-IN-PUBLICATION DATA**

Anania, Michael, 1939–
    In plain sight : Essays / Michael
Anania—1st ed.
      p.  cm.
I. Title.
PS3551.N25I5  1991
814'.54—dc20
ISBN 1–55921–046–X cl         91–16130
                           CIP

Printed in the United States of America
Distributed by Rizzoli International Publications, Inc.

# Contents

# Introduction

I first encountered Michael Anania as a poet; and I think of him still
as a poet, even after having read his disturbingly funny novel, *The
Red Menace*, and the essays collected in this volume. What moves
me most in all of his writing, that is to say, is its language, the way
in which it manages to remain faithful to the homeliness of
colloquial American speech and yet somehow rescues it from
banality, endows it with elegance and grace. Precisely this, however, has been traditionally thought of as the function of poetry. So
why then, I found myself asking as I made my way through these
pieces (pleased and satisfied, yet a little puzzled all the same) has
Anania so often abandoned the formalities of verse to say what he
has to say, *needs* to say? "Obsessions" his subtitle calls the subjects
he treats in this volume.

A clue to why he has done so is to be found, it seems to me, in
the essay included here entitled "Poetry: the remarkable thing is that
there is so much of it." Appropriately enough, though the piece
began as an omnibus review of a year's more serious poetry books,
it was originally published in the *Chicago Tribune*, a popular
newspaper many, perhaps most of whose audience has never read
any poetry at all, and probably never will. In it, in any case, Anania

notes—a little ruefully—that ". . . it generally seems true that more people are writing poetry than reading it."

To be sure, in this piece and several others he deals with writers and writings respected (and almost exclusively read) in the academy; yet he does not condescend to his less educated readers nor adjust his rigorous standards to meet their tastes. Nor does Anania write in the hermetic jargon all too fashionable, these days, in academic circles. Though Anania is himself a college professor with all the proper academic qualifications—including a Ph.D.—he clearly wants to address not just his colleagues but, hopefully everyone—at the very least that mythical ideal representative of everyone whom old fashioned personal essayists used to call "the gentle reader."

It is for this reason, surely, that the range of Anania's subjects is so wide. Just as he finds nothing too highbrow or recondite for his prose meditations, he finds nothing too mundane and commonplace. Indeed, some of the essays in this collection which seemed to me finally the most moving, struck me at first as the most unpromising: dealing with such ostensibly trivial subjects as "Teenspeak" (a topic on which surely too much had been written already), the American love affair with cars (it is one form of eroticism to which I am immune) and neckties (I never wear one myself). Almost miraculously, though, Anania succeeds in making them occasions for truly new insights into such universal, ancient themes as desire and delusion, aspiration and despair.

He is never betrayed, however, into empty abstractions; largely, I believe, because everything he writes is anchored in the real and the immediate. He never forgets, for instance, his own class origins or the places, rural and urban, in which he has, like the rest of us, lived, loved and begotten. It is, of course, Chicago in particular to which he returns again and again: the streets, its people and the writers who have created its myth, from Theodore Dreiser and Carl

Sandburg to Saul Bellow and Nelson Algren. And this seems fitting and proper, since of all the great cities of the world it is the one which seems most to need such writers, as if unsure of precisely what it is—or indeed if it really exists at all—until it has been re-imagined in words.

With such concerns, it is inevitable that Anania's collection turn out to be finally in large part political. We are scarcely surprised therefore to discover at its very center essays on the American West, Spiro Agnew, Hitler and Trotsky. What is surprising, however, is that he treats such subjects with so little self-righteousness, so few standard attitudes of the kneejerk Right or Left. Instead we find what another reviewer had called "tolerance and uncertainty," a prevailing tone of civilized, humane skepticism—along with an immunity to clichés, which is surely this volume's greatest virtue.

LESLIE A. FIEDLER

# I

PART ONE

1

## Myths of the American West:

## Two Views of the Oregon Trail

The man standing beside me is a retired stockyards drover from Sarpy County, Nebraska. The steel-guitar Western twang in his voice is real; so are the stiff curls in the toes of his cowboy boots. When he lifts his straw hat, it leaves a deep sweat-band furrow in his hair that no Sunday-morning douse of Wildroot or Brylcreem will erase. The wrinkles at the back of his neck are as sharply cut as cracks in dry soil. At the end of a small boat landing in front of us, his youngest son and my daughter are dangling night crawlers into the dust-colored waters of the Platte River. The exhaust fan of the bait shop-diner behind us is pumping the air full of the smells of patti-melts and french fries. He points across the water to a stand of cottonwoods. That's his camper, an Apache, half-shaded from the midday sun. Massive corporate farms stretch off in every direction. We are standing on the Overland Trail. All the pioneers, the Mormons, and the forty-niners who set off from Council Bluffs passed by here early in their long journey west, and it is impossible not to transform his camper and the others circled in the trees into covered wagons. This is the same ground, after all, the same slow, murky river, the same flat western horizon, and my companion, who seems more American by half than I do, makes a plausible pioneer. The landscape fills quickly with images from State House panoramas and Hollywood movies, but what I want to hold in my mind with conviction eludes me, as it always has—the sense of distance and empty space that had to have settled on each voyager at about this point in the journey, the sheer awe and terror of it mixed with the hard labor of each day's progress and fashioned by the arduous dream of the infinite possibilities of what awaited him in California or Oregon.

The great overland migration to the Pacific Coast is a primary element in American mythology, and as such, it has been the subject of legend, folklore, political rhetoric, and pure fantasy since the day after the first wagons set off across the plains. It has served as an emblem of national purpose and proof of the American strength of character, and it has been the source for countless novels and hundreds of movies. The imagery of the covered-wagon pioneers has been so fully developed that most of the real, historical journey is lost or deeply buried. Some of the most common depictions of life on the trail are completely inaccurate or hopelessly exaggerated. The picture of the small, single-file wagon train, threading its way across an immense, empty space, is largely false. For most of the period the trail was crowded with wagons, and by 1850 travelers complained about the difficulty of finding empty campsites along the way. Popular accounts have often concentrated on the Platte River segment of the trip for their dramatization of hardship and valor, though the first half of the trail was the easiest. It was referred to as a highway, and some fortunate, well-stocked travelers compared it to a Sunday outing. The most popular image, the circle of wagons on the high plains surrounded by attacking Indians, is perhaps the most erroneous. Hostile encounters on the plains were extremely rare. Ninety percent of the deaths due to Indian encounters occurred in the Far West, beyond South Pass. Pitched battles were almost unheard of, even among documented hostilities, and in the end more Indians were killed than emigrants. Even that stalwart figure of movies and television series, the trail leader scout, is largely a dramatic invention. After a few years, the trail was well enough known and crowded enough to make professional guides and scouts unnecessary.

Historical rendering, as well as popular imagery, varies. Early trail histories are dominated by a need to see the adventure as highly individualistic. Later accounts are often bent on finding a typical trail year and extrapolating a typical chronological narrative. John D. Unruh's *The Plains Across* is an attempt to view the migration as a whole, from 1840, when the first avowed emigrants disembarked, through 1860. It is a massively researched, readable, engaging book, well supplied with illustrations, and rich in anecdotes. The overland experience is the second most thoroughly documented, popular episode in 19th-century American history, exceeded only by the Civil War in the number of surviving journals, diaries, and letters. The overlanders knew they were being historic and left extensive accounts of their adventures. Unruh's mastery of this material is simply amazing. It is apparent in the meticulous development of his major arguments and in the ease with which he balances familiar trail lore with unexpected, even comic detail, to build a more textured sense of the experience than has been given before.

Unruh calls *The Plains Across* "revisionist," and two alterations in our view of the Overland Trail dominate. The first, and most significant, is that the overland venture was not essentially individualistic but was, instead, a cooperative venture, involving westbound travelers with one another, with returning, eastbound "turn-arounds" and traders, with the Indians and the Mormons. What he presents is not "humanity on the loose," as one contemporary called the migration, but an elaborate, evolving system of cooperation. His second major revision involves the attention he gives to the changes the trail and the journey underwent in 20 years. That the emigrants cooperated with one another along the way seems common sensical, but the degree and complexity of interaction is remarkable. Goods and labor were traded fluidly on the trail. A system of messages established along the route so often made use of animal skulls that it was called "the bone express." Messages were left for stragglers; rendezvous were set; and one courtship was carried on through trail-side markers, despite the disapproval of both families. Our image of the hearty isolation of the pioneers is somewhat lessened by Unruh's accounts of the work of doctors, blacksmiths, and barbers along the trail, and by the early development of a fairly reliable mail system that used Indians and "turn-arounds" to carry letters from the wagon trains to friends and families in the East.

The most remarkably documented cooperative relationship on the trail is the one that evolved between the pioneers and the Indians. Early in the migration, the Indians are most often noted for the help they provided the emigrants. Sometimes they served as guides, often as traders. Some tribes improved the trail itself, then traded with the travelers for the right to use their improvements. In the more mountainous portions of the trail, Indians were prized for their ability to swim draft animals across swift rivers, and some diarists said that it was foolhardy to attempt most river crossings without Indian help. The danger from hostile Indians was always exaggerated, and some of the most notorious massacres of the period were pure fabrication. In what is probably the most impressive use of source materials in a generally impressive book, Unruh documents the decline of emigrant-Indian relations at several specific locations. By looking at a sequence of diaries dealing with an Indian bridge, for example, he is able to show how a hostile encounter was created when successive trains complained about tolls, then refused to pay, and, at last, shot at the Indians for having the effrontery to ask for payment at all. The unsuspecting fourth train in this series was attacked without warning and no doubt sent back warnings to those that followed that the Indians thereabouts were dangerous, thus perpetuating the problem. Most diarists, even in the 1850s, when white and Indian relations had suffered through many similar encounters, said that the greatest danger from Indians was theft, not violence. Moviegoers, who have seen thousands of whites and red-skins bite the dust, will be amazed to know that at the end of 20 years along the trail, 362 emigrants and 426 Indians had been killed.

Unruh's sense of the trail as cooperative rather than individualistic is aimed at revising not only our sense of specific overland images and myths but our sense of the cultural importance of the whole adventure. Throughout American history the overland experience has been used to solidify our sense of isolated, individual effort and the isolation of the family unit. If we look back on the trail, crowded with people, wagons running often 12 abreast, with complex interactions taking place at all points, we have a completely different model. What we see is not the fabled abandonment of social and economic institutions but their persistence and flexibility under stress. Even the accounts of what was cast off along the trail change the common view of the pioneer. Chests of heirlooms, rockers, and the tear-stained spinets the movies treat so fondly were cast aside, but so were anvils, bellows, law books, grindstones, and bookcases. Even a diving bell was reported left by the trail near Salt Lake City. One of the most successful Oregon pioneers carried fruit trees the whole way. If we are to judge by what they carried along, the pioneers were expecting to build lives in the West not so different from the ones they left behind.

John Mack Faragher's *Women and Men on the Overland Trail* is a good supplement to Unruh. Faragher is interested in family life on the trail, particularly with the role of women on the frontier. Much of this study is devoted to understanding the population that made up the migration. Most of the emigrants came from farms in the

Near West, and Faragher describes family life and farm labor in the Midwest in the 1840s in great detail. The labor of day-to-day farm life, especially for women charged with cooking, weaving, sewing, gardening, child-bearing, and child-rearing, is almost unimaginable. The trail seems excruciating to us in part because we have had very little sense of the normal work of the people who set out for the West.

Faragher depicts the emigrant wife as someone totally identified with the work of the home. Because of her place in society and marriage, she was denied any real chance of participating in the decision to emigrate. Diaries written by married men on the trail rarely talk of loneliness or isolation. As we have seen, the trail had no shortage of company. Women's diaries complain of loneliness and isolation almost constantly. They were bound to the same duties that kept them busy from dawn to dusk on their abandoned farms, but on the trail these duties had to be compressed into "rest" periods. When the train stopped, the women set to work, cooking, cleaning, and mending, and there was generally a lack of social contact, even in busy trail camps. The common picture of the bonneted pioneer wife seated in a covered wagon while her husband drove the team is also a false one. More often, the women walked behind the wagon, collecting kindling and buffalo chips for the next campfire.

Faragher develops his picture of farm and trail family life from personal accounts, but he also relies heavily on farm statistics and demographic data. The result is generally persuasive and occasionally interesting, but it makes for a slow text, and at times the statistics, however persuasive, stand in the way of his developing a clear sense of the actual lives he is describing. Still, the book is the first effort to deal with the family dynamics of the trail and to focus, specifically, on the women who made the journey. Faragher's conclusion is compatible with the sense of society on the trail in

Unruh. Although the decision to go west meant immense changes for the family, the basic marital relationship was not expected to change at all. The male pioneers expected to transport their family units intact, with all the assignments of work, responsibility, and power unchanged. Some women argued against going: a few flatly refused. Not a single female diarist recounts having initiated the idea. The hope of change was a male prerogative.

Both of these books are valuable to our understanding of the great migration west. Unruh's *The Plains Across* is also vivid and engaging enough to have a chance at changing our images of the trail. It is not at all a bad thing to have in one of America's most cherished myths a potential model for social and economic cooperation, even though we will have to look elsewhere for our models of equivalent flexibilities in marriage and family roles.

2

# Particularities of American Life:

# Two Oral Histories

"The converts was all lined up on the bank about forty or fifty of em. The girls was dressed in white and looked kinda scared. Then the crowd would sing, 'Shall we gather at the river, the beautiful, the beautiful river,' and the line would move down into the water. The girls dresses would float up around their waists, and the preacher would poke em down with his cane. He'd lay his hands on each one . . . and then he'd dip em over backward into the water. As they come up, he'd pat each one on the shoulder and say, 'Sister, you're saved.' . . . That's the way I happened to marry Sally. We was converted at the same meeting and baptized at the same baptizing."

That's Harry Sloan talking. Sloan, a North Carolina tenant tobacco farmer, was interviewed in 1938 by two writers from the WPA's Federal Writers' Project. Like nearly all tenant farmers, Sloan was caught between low tobacco prices and high landlord levies, but his interview is much more than a proof text for an economic history of the rural South. We are listening in as Sloan's stories shape his life, and the talk is so vivid that it is no trouble at all to see a pair of hardened hands moving with the tale, agitated by the righteous sensuality of that luminous baptism, white dresses glowing above brown river water, the preacher's cane poking down at buoyant clouds of white cotton.

The Sloan interview was discovered by Ann Banks among the 150,000 pages of life-history interviews deposited at the Library of Congress at the close of the Federal Writers' Project in 1941. The project was the WPA's attempt to provide employment for writers during the Depression. At its peak, it employed 6,500 people, among them Saul Bellow, Richard Wright, Conrad Aiken, Arna Bontemps, John Cheever, Ralph Ellison, Nelson Algren, May Swenson, and Studs Terkel.

Most of the narratives in *First-Person America* were gathered by the project's folklore division under the directorship of Benjamin Blotkin, and the richness and variety of the archive owe a great deal to Blotkin's influence. He shifted the attention of the folklore section away from the picturesque and the quaint to matters of everyday life. Although the resulting archive provides the largest "oral history" ever undertaken, Blotkin's charge to his writer-interviewers only occasionally involved the topical focus that characterizes most of what we now call oral history. He saw storytelling as one of the folk arts and encouraged his writers to develop their interviews into conversational social occasions in which stories could flourish.

The vividness of Harry Sloan is not unique. There are equally engaging accounts of life on the frontier, of early mining efforts, of packinghouse work in Chicago and stonecutting in Vermont. There are interviews with vaudevillians and medicine-show pitchmen, steelworkers, gold miners, jazz musicians, and prostitutes. In the book's opening section, "Old Times," there are fondly detailed accounts of country dances, Fourth of July picnics, and the festivities that women developed around quilting and berry picking.

Some of these storytellers have a gift for comic exaggeration that suggests Mark Twain and other 19th-century vernacular humorists.

William Moody, a rodeo clown, describes steer riding: "And let it be known that the only difference between riding a steer and a hanging is you've got the noose in your hand—that's all! It's the first jump the steer makes that pops your neck. A man never really knows how long his neck is till he rides a steer. Your neck stretches like an elastic band. With a pair of binoculars you can look down and see if a giraffe parts his hair in the middle or on the side."

A great deal of *First-Person America* concentrates on work and on working conditions, particularly on occupational hazards and diseases. Many of the subjects talk about the problems of union organizing, about women in packinghouses fired for wearing CIO buttons on the job. One steelworker tells of another who fell into a ladle full of molten steel: "He goes pouff into nothing. Then the company buried the guy with the steel until the family got over the accident, or until they moved away. After that the company dug up the metal and used it in making steel."

Among the most impressive interviews is a sequence of life histories collected in Harlem by Ralph Ellison. Ellison's ability to catch the music in the speech of his subjects makes this section particularly lively. Material from these interviews made its way into *Invisible Man*. Other writers in the collection also used their interviews for later work, including Nelson Algren, whose interview with a prostitute contributed to *A Walk on the Wild Side*, and Sam Ross, whose experiences in interviewing Chicago jazz musicians found their way into *Windy City*.

*First-Person America* should become an American classic. It is a monument to Blotkin and the writers in the WPA and a lively historical document. And Banks has provided a survey and an introduction to a great manuscript resource and in her research has made a first step in organizing and cataloguing the archive. But the strength of her book is not, finally, in its vindication of the Writers' Project or even in its historical usefulness. It is in its preservation of the particularities of American life, even in its bleakest moments, that *First-Person America* seems to do its most essential work—tobacco bundles, canning crocks, quilting frames, mining tools, place names, family, friends, life stories carded like fresh wool from the snarl of immediate occasions and spun like new thread while the language hums with invention. In a world increasingly dominated by commercial images and canned laughter, nothing could be more refreshing.

*American Mosaic* is a contemporary oral history. Joan Morrison and Charlotte Ford Zabusky spent four years tape-recording interviews with immigrants, selecting subjects that would give the book the broadest possible coverage of the immigrant experience. Their subjects come from Western Europe, Russia, the Middle East, India, China, Japan, even South Africa and Vietnam. The authors deliberately include immigrants from a broad range of social and economic classes—scientists, writers, and dancers, as well as peasants, refugees, and laborers—and they also attempt to exhibit the range of adaptation and American success with, among others, the stories of a former Secretary of the Treasury and a Polish housekeeper.

A number of the accounts confirm the traditional view of American immigration—of oppressed people in search of political, economic, and racial freedom. The first section shows people who have exchanged oppression for hardship. In the early part of the century, successive waves of immigrants meant new and cheap labor. Here, as in *First-Person America*, there is a sense of the significance of work in people's lives and the overwhelming importance of the development of strong industrial unions.

What is most striking in the stories of the early immigrants is the urgency of the need they felt for education and the range of reading referred to with great fondness by men and women working in hospitals, restaurants, and garment factories. Pauline Newman, who started working at the age of eight in the Triangle Shirtwaist Factory in New York, joined a literary society that had a teacher from the City College visit twice a week. So after ten-hour days in the cutting room, she and her coworkers studied Charles Dickens and George Eliot. There are other stories about education but none quite so damning in its conclusion. Newman became an organizer for the ILGWU and eventually the union's education director. After nearly 80 years of struggle she is discouraged by the amount of time that workers now spend watching television. "We fought so hard for those hours and they waste them. We used to read Tolstoy, Dickens, Shelley, by candlelight, and they watch the 'Hollywood Squares.' "

Other threads run through these narratives. The need to learn English sent some immigrants to night school and others to the funny papers. Some spent hours in theatres watching the same film over and over, trying to make sense of the language. Others found their way into ethnic enclaves.

The longest and most striking narratives in *American Mosaic* dwell on the details of Old World departures. The most dramatic deal with refugees, not only from Hitler and the horrors of World War Two but also from other tyrannies more contemporary and more remote. One of the book's oldest refugees from military displacement is an Armenian who was driven with the entire population of his village into the desert by the Turkish Army in 1915. The most recent are Vietnamese refugees, among them former Premier Nguyen Cao Ky.

The overall effect of *American Mosaic* is of the sustained promise that America has offered the world. Streets paved with gold—that was the impression many early immigrants had as they set out for America. What they found, with a few remarkable exceptions, were struggle and dislocation. The second, and perhaps more important, lesson in these narratives is that the promise consisted largely of unresolved problems. The most successful of these immigrants took part in making up some solutions. All of them served—still serve—to test pronounced though often shakily held American ideals, if only by their resolute presence.

Although they speak often of difficulty and disillusionment, both of these books have an extremely positive feel about them. "Hard times," as Studs Terkel has shown so well, is a conversational form; like the blues, it has its own delight in the telling. There is a complex, plural patriotism here for anyone who wants it—in the flourish of language and personality of *First-Person America* and in the unfailing belief in change that unifies *American Mosaic*. Both have value for historians and ethnologists, but they make exciting, often powerful reading as well. Together, they offer a specific antidote to the excesses of the political year. To ward off platitudes, flag waving, tinsel patriotism, and self-serving Armageddons, take two or three of these interviews before bedtime.

# 3

## Excesses and Boondoggles

To live in a city—any city worth bothering about, at least—is to live with a city's past, not as an idea or an academic exercise but as a day-to-day fact of life, something you can brush elbows with or lean up against waiting for a bus. Despite the efforts of developers and the recent pestilence of condominiums, Chicago's past still juts out at us, texturing our experience in a variety of ways. The obvious landmarks are a part of this, certainly, but as important as landmark preservation is, a city of machine uniformity with a few official landmarks here and there like leftover party favors would have very little touch with its history.

What makes Chicago remarkable is how much of its past has remained in view. Drive through a Southwest or a Northwest Side neighborhood and notice the blocks of frame houses with their front doors a flight of wooden steps above the street, an exposed masonry basement at or just below sidewalk level. The design is a holdover from the period when the city lifted its center up above the lakeside swamp on which it was built. For a while it was thought that all the streets in Chicago would be graded up with fill, and the first of these householders expected the streets to rise up to meet their doorsills. Downtown the play of building surfaces, dark stone against tinted glass, is an interaction of past and present, in styles of

architecture and building materials, certainly, but also in the sense of
what a building meant. The Loop buildings of Sullivan and Adler
and of Burnham and Root are testaments to weight and perma-
nence; the glass-curtained structures of the city's Miesian phase
favor transparent ground levels that make the floors above seem to
float weightlessly in space.

Each wave of development in Chicago has left its marks and
receded, and each represents an idea or an aspiration. Out in the
industrial areas of the city, isolated among train tracks and truck
yards, these same civic gestures in design can be incongruous, even
comic. There are factory buildings on South Ashland Avenue with
bell towers and neoclassical pillars, machine shops with mosaics and
friezes that assert the nobility of gears, ratchets, and pulleys.
Derelict storefronts gather graffiti in two languages under concrete
lion-head cornices or machine-cast *fleurs-de-lis*, the last reminders of
one puff-chested day years ago when a ribbon was cut, an alderman
muttered, a priest blessed, and a dry-goods store was opened.

More than any other city in America, Chicago offers an archaeology of its own past, and you can read in its contours and its
buildings a record of civic pride, commercial arrogance, and public
and private infamy. The elevated train tracks that give the Loop its
name are the last surviving monument to Charles T. Yerkes, a
near-visionary swindler, who built upward because it was the only
direction left for him to extend his monopoly over Chicago's
streetcars. Grant Park rests in part on soil dug from a Loop tunnel
system, a project that the City Council rejected. The tunnels were
cut anyway, legislated by a few artful changes made in a bill
permitting the telephone company the right to bore holes for its
cables. The forgery was apparently committed as the bill passed
from the council chamber to the records office, and it was undone
only after 60 miles of subway had been completed and a large
stretch of lakefront east of the Illinois Central tracks had been filled.

There was a scandal, of course, but no one was convicted of anything: Money was made and progress served.

Perhaps it is the scale of both civic-minded planners and swindlers that leaves us such large evidence of their work. From its first period of growth before the Fire of 1871 through the explosive period of building that followed, Chicago has been the setting for grand schemes. The city that raised the level of its streets also turned its river around, redrew the lines of its lakeshore several times, and invented the single determining feature of the modern cityscape, the skyscraper. The characters who managed these enormous gestures have a grandeur all their own. From captains of industry and princes of commerce to crooked politicians, gangsters, and madams, Chicago history is filled with larger-than-life characters. In some ways the city seems to breed them or at least give them the right-size stage on which to play. Perhaps it is because Chicago has always been in the process of becoming something that it invites and cultivates such figures. Certainly, it is the unsettled, unfinished quality of the place that has led writers to feel that it wants a single metaphor to characterize it.

Emmett Dedmon's *Fabulous Chicago* is an anecdotal history of the city. Although it adequately sketches the city's development in terms of population, politics, business, and industry, the center of its attention is on character and anecdote. Dedmon concentrates on a few individuals in each period of the city's past, seeing other, broader social and economic matters chiefly as they relate to the people and events that hold his attention, large figures in grand or notorious settings. The result is a highly readable, entertaining, and extremely quotable tour of Chicago history.

*Fabulous Chicago* is at its best when it is treating the slightly dubious characters of Chicago politics and society. Dedmon has a way with social excess and boondoggling. He spins a good Everleigh sisters yarn and treats characters like Bathhouse John Coughlin and Big Bill Thompson with a wry genius that leaves all of their excesses and contradictions in place for the reader to enjoy. Of the earlier portraits, the fullest and most successful is his extended treatment of Long John Wentworth, Chicago's mayor in the late 1850s and early 1860s. Wentworth was a giant man who believed in direct action. He led police raids himself and conducted fire brigades. After deciding that the clutter of awnings and shop signs on State Street was both unsightly and dangerous, he sent out squads of police with wagons to tear them down and stack them on the prairie at the edge of town.

Throughout his history Dedmon also scrupulously traces the development of Chicago society, and although this is not the feature of the book that I found most engaging, it is interesting to see the awkward moccasin-and-deerskin-leggings socials of the frontier period evolve, by one self-conscious turn after another, into the awesome entertainments orchestrated by Mrs. Potter Palmer at the end of the 19th century.

The greatest deficiency of the history is implied in the book's title. This is *fabulous* Chicago, and what is passed over here is the unfabled life of the city and how it evolved. Dedmon faithfully records the major labor conflicts in Chicago's past—the Haymarket Riot, the Pullman Strike, and the Republic Steel Strike—but there is very little sense offered here of life of the working classes in Chicago. Very little is shown of the situations of rural immigrants to the city and their dilemmas, either in the 1890s when country girls like Dreiser's Sister Carrie came looking for a new life or in the waves of "cleaned out" farmers characterized in Frank Norris's *The Pit* who began moving here in 1900.

Missing, too, is an informing view of early-20th-century immigrant Chicago or a view of black Chicago, around which sharp color lines had been drawn by 1912. In some ways, of course, I am being unfair to Dedmon and his clear purposes. He touches, however briefly, on most of these things as they pertain to the fabled lives he does treat, but it is worth wondering how much of the Chicago we know is the gift of labor and of suffering, of steady immigrant determination and reliable bloc voting, and it is impossible not to wonder at the mean limitations of backyard tenements in the midst of so much fabled conspicuous consumption and such charming skullduggery.

*Fabulous Chicago* was first published in 1953 and has served as a popular history of the city ever since. This enlarged edition includes events of Chicago's recent past and deals in some detail with the political career of Mayor Daley. This final portion is inevitably less entertaining than the book's earlier sections, not because Dedmon does not know his material but because all of us know it, perhaps too well. Anecdotes are best when they seem to drift at some distance from their consequences. Also, the characters of our own period—with the clear exception of Mayor Daley, as larger-than-life a Mayor as Chicago has ever produced—have not yet sorted themselves out. Hefner is here, to be sure, Bunnies and all. So are Muhammad Ali, Martin Luther King, Jr., and Jane Byrne. It is a responsibly laid-out quick tour.

Thirteen years ago, when Red Grooms did his great Chicago construction, he gave us two colossal figures—Mayor Daley astride City Hall, facing east, and Hugh Hefner, pipe clenched in his teeth, heading down Michigan Avenue. Both have the wild expansiveness required to keep company with the other central characters in Dedmon's fabulous city, and both attest to a kind of continuity in the city's ability to act as host and background for the extravagant.

Anyone interested in Chicago history should read this book, though most serious Chicago buffs probably already have. Others interested in reading that code of surfaces we pass through every day and seeing there signs of a wild, raucous, and even occasionally noble past should read it, as well. It is especially useful as a companion to Harold Mayer and Richard Wade's *Chicago: Growth of a Metropolis*, with its wealth of pictures and its fine architectural commentary.

4

## Breweries and Bad Men:

## On Prohibition

On summer evenings, sitting on high-backed kitchen chairs pulled out into the yard, my grandfather and his friends would reminisce about Prohibition in sweet litanies full of judges, policemen, speakeasies, fast cars, old friends, and old enemies. Diagrams of stills were scratched into the ground between them—cookers, coils, even the inverted light bulbs they would suspend into the finished liquor to give it a quick aging and take away some of its bite. Recipes were called up like alchemical formulas—a little rye for flavor, mahogany chips to add a touch of color at the end. It was clearly the best of their lives, something cherished like the thought of home. From a second, wider circle around them, younger men, uncles mostly, would venture occasional memories, testing themselves against the inner circle, finding a place—a storefront where the stuff was sold, barbershop back rooms, a key garage, road-houses south of town. Scattered at the edges of these rings of men, my cousins and I would sit and listen, never quite certain of when it all happened or what it meant, assured only by the tone of the occasion that these were high times and great deeds, part of a magical world that was somehow lost to the Great Depression.

There was never a hint that anything criminal or dishonorable was being discussed. The subjects were skill, wit, friendship, and adventure. Before the country went dry, these men were industrial laborers and railroad workers. After repeal, they slipped back into a largely idle work force and the WPA. Only the Second World War would put their working lives back together again, but plainly it would never be the same. For a while, they had been entrepreneurs. A few made enough money to buy little bits of city property; one or two held on to restaurants and bakeries through the Depression years. There were no great fortunes made or lost. What gave the period its shimmer was not wealth but freedom, an unexpected liberation from economic and social imperatives. The giddy freedom that illegality gave flappers and their beaus had a counterpart in the escape that Prohibition's opportunities gave these men from the foundry and the sweatshop. If they hadn't become respectable businessmen, they had, at least, become businessmen—self-employed, hard working, in turn cautious and daring, competitive, and self-reliant.

What is most ironic (and the excuse for this nostalgia) is that my grandfather and his friends were part of the population Prohibition was most directly set against. They were urban Catholic industrial workers, the most common victims in temperance melodramas. They were part of the great wave of immigration at the beginning of the century, and so were part of the shift of American life toward urban industrial centers in the North and East. The American temperance movement, from its beginnings in the late 19th century until repeal, was Midwestern and Southern, rural and Protestant. Its constituency was similar to that of the Populist movement, and after the Populists lost many of their programs to the garrulousness of the two major parties, Prohibition became the gathering point for agrarian discontent in America. In 1869 the Prohibition Party was founded as an aspiring third party. Though it was occasionally influential, it was not very successful. By 1890 it had succeeded in electing just one candidate to Congress, a Minnesotan who had been slated as well by the Agrarian Alliance. The most successful temperance organization was the Anti-Saloon League. The league shared the Prohibition Party's goal of a country made dry by constitutional amendment, but its greatest gains politically were made by shifting its aim toward the saloon, an urban symbol, every town's gate to hell.

Sean Dennis Cashman's *Prohibition: The Lie of the Land* deals in detail with the work of the Anti-Saloon League and Wayne Wheeler, its most powerful head. The discussion is unexpectedly timely. The league's history is a study in special-interest politics and could serve as a model for morality politics in America, from anti-comic-book crusades to the Moral Majority. By concentrating, first, on saloons, the league relieved the anxieties of some of its most cautious supporters and gave politicians an area of ambiguity they could live with right up to the moment that Woodrow Wilson's veto of the Volstead Act was overridden in Congress in 1919. The initial attack was on saloons, their hours, locations, and their economic ties to breweries, but the league was also active in pushing for dry initiatives in individual states.

Even by contemporary standards, the league's lobbying powers would seem awesome. With its threat of political censure, it manipulated several Presidents and Congresses, and its influence on state and local elections across the country was unmatched by any other group. "Wet" congressmen were targeted for defeat; "dry" candidates were given political and financial support. The tactic worked in two ways; either the "wets" were replaced by "drys" or "wet" politicians agreed to give lip service to the league's immediate goals. In the congressional election of 1914, the league fielded more than 50,000 speakers nationwide at a cost of $2.5 million. In the course of its campaigning for successive forms of prohibition, it spent $35 million. It used the need for grain and a clear-eyed populace during the First World War to justify the first

Federal restriction on alcohol and took advantage of nationalistic sentiments against Germans to extend the attack on brewers of German extraction. Prohibition violations were an excuse for tightened immigration laws in 1922. Foreign sources for supplies of smuggled liquor confirmed a general isolationism. Fundamentalist anti-Catholicism found new extremes in the campaigns against Al Smith, whose argument that Prohibition needed reform made him a "wet." And the temperance movement, in general, had a long, if cautious, alliance with the Ku Klux Klan. Eventually, the broader, fundamentalist agenda of many of the Prohibitionists found its way into national policy.

From our historical perspective, Prohibition seems to have been doomed from the start. The changes in American life that the Christian rural coalition for temperance hoped to forestall were accelerated by the economic booms of the 1920s. The 18th Amendment didn't save the country from immorality and corruption; it extended both. At the end of its long series of battles and connivances, the league and its supporters gave the country an unenforceable law that had never really been tested with the people. During the twenties, the per capita consumption of alcohol grew. Saloon drinking had been a recourse for the lower classes; speakeasy drinking became an amusement for all classes. Women, who had been excluded from most saloons, were welcomed in speaks and nightclubs. We owe to Prohibition the invention of the cocktail, nightclub entertainment, a significant part of the development of jazz, and, in its modern form, at least, organized crime.

Political corruption reached new heights. In a famous episode in Cicero, Illinois, rival gangs bought and controlled rival political parties. The Democratic election commissioner, in the service of one mobster, struck the names of Republicans from the register. In retaliation, the rival gang, Al Capone's, kidnaped Democratic election workers and a large number of voters and held them prisoner in Chicago until the polls were closed. Politicians, judges, policemen, and Federal agents were on the take in every big city in the country. Chicago's gangs were famous for their flamboyance and their open warfare, but the corruption that made Chicago famous was pandemic. During the Harding Administration the Justice Department reportedly received seven million dollars in payoffs from bootleggers, and a number of Harding's Ohio associates ran a Washington, D.C., speakeasy that sold liquor delivered daily by Federal agents after it had been confiscated by the Prohibition Unit. Hypocrisy over Prohibition had become a political habit, closely enforced by a vigilant league; corruption was an easy second step. Simple, rural moralism had given way to a general cynicism about the law.

Sean Cashman, in addition to outlining the rural backgrounds of Prohibition, argues that American political life was, in the period, characterized by inventions. Inventions took the place of solutions to problems. As absurd as it now seems, Prohibition was no more strange than other efforts to invent, or declare, change. The Kellogg-Briand Pact outlawed war; the demand of war-loan repayments and German reparations was finally dealt with by a plan that had American banks giving German banks money to give to the Allies to return to American banks. The gesture changed no one's economy; Adolf Hitler was not robbed of a volatile issue, but a settlement was declared. The Volstead Act set about declaring (or inventing) a change in the habits of society, and its proponents were so committed to change by declaration that they themselves often argued against funds for enforcement.

Cashman includes a lengthy discussion of the growth of gangs in Chicago and New York. It is familiar territory, but his research is thorough. There were gangs and gangsters before Prohibition, of course, but in its own characteristically absurd way Prohibition gave them stature. Al Capone became an international figure. Even now, more than 50 years after the St. Valentine's Day Massacre,

Europeans, when they hear the word "Chicago," still clutch imagined tommy guns (or "Chicago pianos") and say, "Al Capone . . . eh . . . eh . . . eh . . . eh." As interesting as the rise of the gangs and their eventual syndication is the place the gangster took in popular culture. Gangster movies became Hollywood's most popular fare, and though movie morality required eventual punishment, gangsters were the heroes, the only indigenous hero invented after the cowboy. Like the cowboy, the gangster was inextricably bound to his environment. The cowboy belonged to the West, the gangster to the city; and in the best of the genre, the city, with its harsh lines and deep shadows, is at least a second lead. The fascination with gangsters, from *Scarface* to *The Godfather*, is modern and urban and involves a complex recognition of the limits of personal action and the costs it exacts in brutality and isolation. The essential exchange is between moral behavior and action, self-interested and direct, proceeding from simple loyalties.

Perhaps in America change is always preceded by reactionary fervor, as though we see the future more perfectly than we ever admit and invent elaborate systems to forestall it. The change that the temperance coalition was fighting was inevitable. If anything, Prohibition hurried it along, advancing national cynicism, even creating the conditions in which its cynical antiheroes might flourish. We are, at the moment, in another period of fundamentalist fervor—over sexual behavior, abortion, welfare, even children's books—and once again the plan seems to be to lobby by moral intimidation for legislated morality. The example of Prohibition offers a number of cautions. Moral politics usually comes to us with simple, high-minded goals, but it frequently takes its emotional force from deeper resentments with much broader implications.

Cashman's history is thorough and readable, but it lacks the vividness that oral history has given to much recent American historical writing. It's not just the voices of my grandfather and his friends that I miss here, but the fascination with detail that their talk always involved. In the necessary presentation of policy and strategy, the essential, quotidian Prohibition seems to have been overlooked. Reading through *Prohibition: The Lie of the Land*, I found myself regretting the absence, in Chicago at least, of a good Prohibition monument, something infamous like the St. Valentine's Day garage or the Four Deuces Club or tawdry like Capone's Hotel Metropole, with space for a few Prohibition artifacts: a copper-kettle still, a hand-operated bottle capper, a barrel lid with a light socket, perhaps, and a few handfuls of mahogany chips.

# II

PART TWO

# 5

## Teenspeak

I was at least two years into the business of being the parent of a teen-ager before I realized that to some extent this war of attrition was caused by a language barrier. I was speaking ordinary, adult English. My daughter had been raised to speak the same language. By the age of 12 she had become quite good at it. She could conduct conversations, answer complex questions, tell jokes, and give directions. Within a year, though, she had changed languages; she had begun to practice Teenspeak.

Teenspeak is difficult to cope with because although it is a different language, it has an English vocabulary. The result is that you can easily believe that you understand it. It all seems to make sense. You nod and smile, sit back, open your newspaper, and believe that you know what has been said. Later, when you discover that nothing you think you were told is true, you get angry and call a conference to settle on the appropriate punishment for the deception you think has occurred. Punishment—or the threat of punishment—breeds anger and recrimination. Somewhere upstairs a door is slammed, which you take to be an affront to your authority. In fact, the slammed door is one of the three most common forms of Teenspeak punctuation. The other two are the stamped foot and the abruptly turned head, both of which are also easily mistaken for affronts to your authority. If you take these gestures seriously, there will be another conference and another cycle of anger.

A rudimentary understanding of Teenspeak can make a parent's life a little more comfortable. It won't make it better. Nothing will. This is not a war you win. I am assured by friends whose children are now ambassadors, bank presidents, and Nobel Prize winners that at some point it ends. It ends, I gather, in much the same way that a head cold ends. One day you notice that you're not sniffling any more.

Whether that day comes before or after the Nobel Prize is awarded is still not clear. Here, then, like a pillow fluffed under your head or a glass of hot lemonade, is an introduction to Teenspeak.

There is no point in trying to deal with the language that teen-agers use with one another ("boss," "cool," "bad," "awesome," "bogus," "tubular"). By the time any of us learns this vocabulary, it will have changed. Also, these words don't really have specific meanings. Instead, each has a variety of meanings. What is meant by the Teenspeaker is indicated by pitch, tone, and duration of the sound—a little like Chinese. Most parents encounter the tonal dimension of teen language domestically when dealing with the inflections of the term "All right." In response to an ordinary request, like "Take out the garbage," "All right" can mean: (a) *Don't bother me;* (b) *Did somebody cut off your legs?;* (c) *I deeply resent the authority you have over me, but I acknowledge it and will take out your stupid garbage;* (d) *Out of affection for you and respect for your age, I will take out the garbage;* or (e) *OK.* These variations are meant to be understood and to infuriate you. If the garbage in question is not actually overflowing, it is occasionally possible for you to appreciate the way that your otherwise unsubtle kid can subtly move from meaning (a) through meaning (e) in one short conversation.

Depending on tone, the word "Great" can mean *Great, Not that again,* or *You've ruined my life.* The word "Sure," however, never indicates simple agreement as it does in ordinary English. Depending on the duration the word is given, "Sure" means *That's just what I'd expect of an old person, You don't know what you're talking about,* or *You've ruined my life.* "Yeah" has the same range of meanings as "Sure," but in the case of "Yeah" the briefest version has the most devastating intent. "Great," "Sure," and "Yeah" are common exit lines, and exits require punctuation, so it's "Great [*slam*]," "Sure [*stamp*]," and "Yeah [*abruptly turned head*]." When used in a dramatic exit and punctuated in this manner, all three words mean *You've ruined my life.* Before you allow yourself to be overcome with guilt, you should know that in the common Teenspeak expression "You've ruined my life," the phrase "my life" refers to the next 45 minutes.

Of the words whose meaning teen-agers manipulate by shifts in tone, the most important for parental survival is "Oh." When it is pronounced with a rising pitch and a quick, almost breathless stop, "Oh" is the involuntary warning sign of an impending expenditure, as in "Oh, I lost my retainer" ($90) or "Oh, I need a new computer book" ($23.50). Optimists have argued that this warning signal indicates that somewhere inside your teen-ager there is still a vestige of the sweet, generous child you once knew. Cynics say that it is no more sweet in intent than the rattle on a snake.

The extended hardships of life with a teen-ager—the ones that steal a whole evening or wipe out a whole Sunday—come from perfectly ordinary expressions that have their own Teenspeak meanings. Simple remarks almost never mean what they seem to mean. "I've cleaned my room," for example, means *The mess that was in the middle of my room has now been moved to the edges of my room.*

"I've cleaned my desk" means *The mess that was on my desk is now in the middle of my room.* As a general rule, it is safe to assume that no statement including the words "my room" means what you think. "My room's too hot" means *I'm not ready to go to bed.* So does "My room's too cold." Statements having to do with clothing are equally dangerous. "I have nothing to wear" means *The laundry I have been hiding for the past two weeks is now so well hidden even I can't find it.* "Everybody's wearing them" means *I saw them on a heavy-metal rock video on MTV.* "It's not that cold" means *I've lost my parka.* "There's not that much snow" means *Only geeks wear boots.* "Can I borrow your umbrella?" means *Do you realize that with this umbrella I will complete the collection of umbrellas at the bottom of my locker?*

The word "plan" should also put you on your guard. To a teen-ager a plan is any vague notion associated with the near future. A plan becomes definite when the vague notion has been mentioned to at least one other teen-ager and sanctified by the ritual word "like." If one place-name has been mentioned, the plan is absolutely definite. When a plan becomes absolutely completely definite, it means that you are driving. Statements involving the word "plan" are all emotionally charged. "I have plans for Saturday night" means *I am now reserving the right to be angry and depressed if something wonderful doesn't happen to me on Saturday night.* "You've ruined my plans," of course, means *You've ruined my life.*

If we were lucky, most of us had parents who paid attention to what we did in school only at report-card time or if we got into trouble. In contemporary America we have been convinced that we should be involved with our children's education. This is a notion advanced by teachers who quite wrongly believe that they are suffering alone. As an involved parent you are supposed to ask questions and encourage dialogue. Asking questions and encouraging dialogue puts you in the way of another wave of Teenspeak. "How was school today?" is a modest effort at discharging your responsibility. The usual answer is "OK." "OK" in this context means *Don't ask.* If you find this answer unsatisfactory, you can say, "What did you do in school today?" The answer is always "Nothing." This is one of the few times when teen-agers say exactly what they mean. If you allow yourself to be drawn further into the subject of school; you become concerned about homework. "Have you done your homework?" you ask. The answer is "Yes," which means *Yes, No,* or *Don't ask.*

The next step is foolhardy. "When did you do your homework? You've been watching television ever since you got home." The answer is "I did it in study hall." This means *Since I have already spent an hour at school pretending to do this work, why should I go upstairs and spend another hour pretending to do it?* Variations include "I don't have any homework," which means *I forgot my book,* and "She never gives homework," which means *I've lost my book.* "I don't know when it's due" means *It's due tomorrow.* "Can you help me with this?" and "You promised to help me with this" means *It was due today.* "You have to sign this" means *Read it if you insist but don't say I didn't warn you.*

Some of the strange behavior of teen-agers is created by an important biological imperative. Teen-agers, like hummingbirds, must eat five times their weight in food each day. The result is an added difficulty in understanding. Much of what they say to you is acoustically distorted by the inside of the refrigerator. Even if you master the refrigerator echo, what you hear is still coded Teenspeak. "What's for dinner?" means *Why are you just standing around when you could be feeding me?* "There's nothing to eat" means *We're all out of junk food.* "I haven't had anything to eat" means *Hamburgers, french fries, and milkshakes don't count.* "Is this all we're having?" means *Green things don't count.* "What's the problem? I just made myself a sandwich" means *The leftover pot roast you were planning to use for tonight's dinner fit nicely between two pieces of bread.*

As a contemporary, involved parent, you are supposed to discuss things with your teen-ager. The alternatives can be seen regularly on the *Movie of the Week*. According to television, all the unspeakable tragedies of modern domestic life are caused by parents who fail to discuss things with their teen-agers; so whatever happens, have discussions. Do not be too upset, though, if your attempts at discussion leave you confused and frustrated. Teenspeak does not change just because the subject is serious. When you raise a problem, the common response is "I'll take care of it," which means *I am willing to pretend that I take this seriously if you are willing to pretend you believe me.* "I don't want to talk about it" indicates that you've touched a nerve and means *If you insist on talking about it, I'm going to do a ten-minute soap-opera imitation and give you a headache.* "That's not how we do things now" and "You don't understand" don't really have meanings. Both are tactical ploys meant to weaken your resolve by forcing you to think about your age. "You think everything is dangerous" means *I understand that when you get older your bones get brittle.* "Janet's mother said it was OK with her" means *Janet thinks that if you agree, she can get her mother to agree.* "I never get to do anything" means *If you make me stay home, you'll be sorry.* "Trust me" means *Experience is less important than blind faith.*

If you insist on bringing a serious discussion to some kind of conclusion, you can say, "Do you understand what I'm saying?" The answer is invariably "Sure," which means as we've already noted, *That's just what I'd expect from an older person, You don't know what you're talking about,* or *You've ruined my life.* If you're the sort of person who won't take "Sure" for an answer, you are likely to persist and in so doing leave yourself open for a "Whatever." "Whatever" is one of Teenspeak's ultimate remarks. It means *Why are you still talking when it would be obvious, even to a casual observer, that I have stopped listening?*

Teenspeak has individual variations—twists and turns invented by an individual or a discrete cadre of teen-agers, but this introduction should allow you to make some sense, however tenuous, out of what's happening to you. Do not, however, allow yourself to believe that you understand completely. Occasionally all teen-agers slip back into ordinary speech. They do this to trap you or because they forget. (Being incomprehensible is hard work, after all.) If they catch you translating when you should just be listening, it's an incredible victory for their side. As a reward, they get to say, "You never listen to me."

6

## The Child's Guerrilla War with the City

On hot summer days when the fire hydrant at 18th and Union is opened, an iron bar is wedged against the spout so that the water sprays out into a long, broad fan. Children dance under its bright plumage. Somewhere in the Department of Streets and Sanitation gauges fall. At five, six, and ten, affably urgent newscasters give a few seconds of concern to water pressure. Officials are quoted, and a film clip of children running through illicit water captures the screen.

This annual episode has about it some of the basic elements of the relationship between children and cities. The play here is both primary and ingenious. It is hard to imagine a spray nozzle more efficient or economical than that flat iron bar on South Union Street; certainly no showerhead could manage such a graceful arc. The fact that opening a hydrant is generally illegal and slightly dangerous is also important: In the child's guerrilla war with the adult world, such skirmishes feed his need for risk and excitement. Even society's mixed response is typical. When children come into general social view, they do so as problems, registered on statistical gauges that measure crime, poverty, educational failure, vandalism, and disease as remotely as water-pressure gauges measure what happens at fire hydrants. Yet the images of children at play delight and divert us, if only momentarily.

The hydrant scene is an American urban icon, an obligatory part of every photo-essay about the city; it has a place alongside renderings of the old swimming hole and the barefoot boy with straw hat and bamboo fishing pole. The child at the hydrant wins as we might wish to, beating both the heat and the system by taking what is there with defiance and unrestrained gaiety.

Colin Ward's new book, *The Child in the City*, describes the American fire hydrant, juxtaposing anecdotes and photographs of hydrants with accounts of children's use of canals in Manchester and the squabble that lasted through the first 30 years of the century over London boys swimming in the Hyde Park Serpentine. Ward is a British authority on urban education, and much of the material in his book deals directly with English cities. Still, there is an effort, largely successful, both in the text and in the photographs, to include children and cities throughout the world.

It is an uncommon book. At first glance it looks like a picture book with too much text, but the text is lively and engaging. Ward makes use of a broad range of sociological and anthropological material, reviewing recent literature concerning urban children and sketching historical contexts as he goes. For Ward, the fusion of picture book and essay is essential. Most essays about the city child leave their readers sinking into a fully justified gloom; pictures of children have a completely different effect. However bleak the conditions they document, they have an unmistakable vitality, sparks of ingenuity, and even joy. Without that second view, says Ward, no presentation of the city child is complete. The problem for city planners, educators, and architects alike lies in reclaiming the city without foreclosing the life of the child. Sadly, except for occasional parks and formulaic school yards, children are simply not considered to be important in most city plans. The modern commercial city, Ward points out, is contrived to serve employed white-collar adults who go places by car.

The book's opening chapter, "Paradise Lost?," concerns the differences for children between the contemporary city and cities of the past. Some obvious forms of exploitation of children have been eliminated, and the staggering mortality rates from disease have been drastically cut, but in Ward's view there have also been losses. City life for the child has become more restrictive. Because so much of the most densely child-populated city is failing, the variety of experience and activity available to the child has diminished. As neighborhoods collapse, the safe range of a child's movement contracts, and the often genial familiarity of neighborhood commerce disappears.

When I was a child, my immediate neighborhood had six family-owned grocery stores, two ice houses, three drugstores, a Jewish bakery, a black taxi-company garage, a pop-bottling plant, a chicken house, a junkyard where we could sell newspapers and flattened tin cans, a Goodwill store, a fish house, seven taverns, three storefront churches, a ragman, a scissors man, a pawnshop, a dry cleaners, a brewery, four wonderfully chaotic filling stations, two barbershops, a lot full of junked cars, a warehouse that stored rock salt, two witches, one clairvoyant, and a beauty parlor. Almost nothing survives today; people shop by car at supermarkets and discount drugstores. There is no way to annoy a chain-store manager into giving you a bagel to go away, and there are no barrels of dried beans at checkout counters where children can prospect for loose change. More importantly, when it died, the languid, small store took with it the child's chance to experiment with commerce.

Where I live now, there are two stores in easy walking distance for a child: One is a Mini-Mart in a gas station nestled in a deadly half-acre of cars and gas pumps; the other is a failing supermarket-liquor store where the candy bars are kept behind a high counter with the half pints. It may be just as well. Inflation has driven younger children out of the economy anyway. The few remaining returnable bottles in the world still bring just two cents; penny candy no longer exists and a nickel candy bar costs 25 cents plus tax.

The most destructive feature of the modern city environment for children—perhaps for us all—is the automobile. The car is the major hazard to children's health. It dominates the streets where most children play, and its necessities dominate, as well, the designs of cities. Children are killed and maimed by cars at an incredible rate. Their access to their environment is constricted by the hazards of the streets, and younger children in dense residential areas have their view of the world walled off by parked cars. Children lack the essential mobility of a car-oriented culture, an adult mobility that has allowed commerce to be increasingly centralized at hazardous distances. Ward, who is concerned throughout his text with the role of education in the city, wonders at the effectiveness of schools that attempt to "foster freedom and independence inside the school" when the world outside has made independence and freedom of movement increasingly inappropriate and dangerous. He notes that in the 1960s the rate of adult pedestrian casualties in automobile accidents increased by nine percent and the rate for children increased 52 percent.

Ward and his assemblage of photographs remind us of the abilities that children have for making niches in the city for their play. They take what's left over and "colonize" it, appropriating doorways, alleys, gutters, stoops, whatever is available. There are wonderful photo sequences on cardboard boxes, climbing, and the uses of railings, and he includes a partial list of street games. Ward argues for a city in which the ingeniousness of children can flourish without hazard, a city in which they can participate. Although he recognizes the need for parks and play areas, children cannot be counted on to follow the prescriptions of planners even when their plans are good. His final argument is for a "shared city" in which children's claims to the space they inhabit are considered and met, and he argues persuasively that a city in which the claims of children to safely share its space were met would be better for the rest of us, as well. This is a passionate, well-argued book full of interesting and occasionally startling material. The photographs are a joy to look at, though many are less than beautiful. Ward's concluding argument is not really utopian. He is asking only that we become as ingenious with the spaces we control as our children are with their leftover bits and pieces.

7

## Small-Town Swan Song

Years ago I caught a ride across Iowa with an old farmer in a dusty pickup truck. He wore a straw field-hat and bib overalls, and had a pint of whiskey twisted into a paper sack between his legs. A good way west of Des Moines we came on the first open stretch of interstate highway between Illinois and California. He stopped the truck, turned south on a two-lane county road, and went five miles out of his way to the next state highway headed east. I asked him why he didn't take the interstate. "Won't use the damned thing," he said, "never will. Pretty soon, every state in this country's gonna be hangin' off one of them things, like so much wash on a line. Be the end of all these little towns. The end of farmin', too." Well, farming has gone on, after a fashion, but the small towns are mostly dead or dying, their place as the center of rural life lost to the ease and regimen of limited-access travel, their moral insularity washed over by television. And sometimes it does seem that the states of American's Midwest flap like laundry in the breeze, detached from the land and its strange social and personal influence.

The small town—the Midwestern small town, in particular—is an American icon. Politicians and cultural chauvinists still hold up its image to us on ceremonial occasions as a measure of America at its best. Intimate, familiar, and supportive, it is the supposed cradle of the basic values of family, home, and community, a nostalgia we do not so much share as cooperatively concoct out of our dreams of a world not yet completely gone wrong. Cities teem and seethe; suburbs sprawl; but small towns drowse beneath sentinel water towers and grain elevators. Back behind Main Street, quiet residential streets named for the first Presidents politely intersect with streets named for American shade trees. There is still a Sabbath there and a washday, and the Johnson house is still owned by somebody named Johnson. It is a world of aprons and consoling repetitions, the ancestral home of "Aw, shucks," "Golly," and "Gee whillikers," where *people* (as in "What will *people* think?") are still a moral force.

A great deal of American literature has been involved in stripping away the placid moral mask of the small town. We have in fiction and poetry a map of the distressed Midwestern psyche from Winesburg, Ohio, to Spoon River in Illinois, Gopher Prairie in Minnesota, and Lone Tree in Nebraska. In this literature, the small town isolates and confines, and the shared values and intense familiarity, which can seem so consoling from a distance, readily become the instruments of a much more keenly enforced despair. The effect of literature's inside view—from inside character looking desperately out—has been iconoclastic, and when small towns still mattered as a real force in American life, Sherwood Anderson and Sinclair Lewis were the subjects of vehement condemnation and angry denial.

Garrison Keillor's *Lake Wobegon Days* wants its small town both ways, as a nostalgic reconstruction of a better world and as an inside view of that world's failings, a mixture of affection and displaced anger that is meant to be held together by gentle wit. It doesn't quite work, although there's a great deal of fun and genuine humor along the way. Lake Wobegon is the Minnesota town that Keillor invented for his monologues on American Public Radio's *A Prairie*

*Home Companion*, "the little town that time forgot . . . where all the women are strong, all the men are good-looking, and all the children are above average," a version of his own childhood town, obviously, but with an invented history and a present sheltered by memory from too much change.

Some of the best and funniest writing in the book is in the chapters that invent Lake Wobegon's history. In Keillor's account, unlike the rest of the fabled Middle America that was discovered and settled by a combination of courage and steadfastness, Lake Wobegon is the product of a century and a half of misadventure, error, and bullheadedness. Its first white man, a French priest, was probably driven off by mosquitoes before he reached the eventual town site. The second, an Italian explorer and poet, briefly hoped that the lake was the headwaters of the Mississippi. He was wrong and knew it almost immediately. The town was finally founded because a Boston Unitarian missionary, Prudence Alcott, set out to central Minnesota with a plan to convert the Indians by means of interpretive dance. The account of Prudence and her party and the return of James Francis Watt, one of her companions, to found New Albion College there is wonderful, as is the sad history of the college itself. Founded on invented credentials with funds from a clever land speculator, it ultimately falls victim to bad weather and impending bears. Keillor's ear for 19th-century ballyhoo is excellent, and the parodies of certainty and high-mindedness in his versions of Watt's lectures and poems give this section of the book the feel of pure invention and absolute authenticity.

The pattern of error set down by the founding fathers continues throughout the town's history. The Norwegians, who make up much of the town's population, arrived by mistake; so did the Germans. The Sons of Knute, the principal fraternal organization, never quite gets anything right, except the annual pool to guess the date on which a car driven out on the lake in winter will sink to the bottom in spring, an event that commemorates one of the Sons' having driven out there one winter by mistake.

This habit of error is very funny, but as it is extended into the present and near-present of the town and its characters, it is also limiting. For Keillor, the lingering monologist, the exploration of a character tends to end with his or her notable mistake; like a carefully forestalled punch line, the defining mistake slowly but inexorably has its way. Rather than having characters proceed, three-dimensionally, from their mistakes, they proceed to them and stop, taking their place in Lake Wobegon's gallery of lovable lunks. There are exceptions—Keillor himself, most notably, whose confessions about his own misperceptions and awkwardness give the book some of its charm and offer some sense of development.

Keillor's characters, though largely undeveloped, live in a wonder of detail. Their cars are all faithfully rendered; so are their overalls and their painfully bland dinners. Lunch at the Chatterbox Café is given an extraordinary, if not an appetizing, description, as are the drinks at the Sidetrack Tap. The anti-institutional Protestantism of Keillor's own family is presented down to the last scriptural license-plate holder. It is this welter of detail, fondly turned, held, and turned again, that gives the nostalgia that informs the whole enterprise its momentum and still another kind of charm, the obsessive precision of long-held, though battered, affections.

There are a few moments of accusation in the book. The most extended comes from a Wobegoner who returns from the East for an autumn visit determined to nail 95 theses of his own to the door of the Lutheran church. Instead, as his defining error, he leaves them at the newspaper office, where they languish under other forgotten bits of paper, never published and, despite their author's many letters, never returned. The 95 theses, minus a few lost over the years and a few obliterated by coffee stains, are reproduced in a long footnote. They are a detailed condemnation of family, church, and town that finally stutters into a series of numbered *Damns*. Another returning child brings her husband along. He sits in the family parlor shut out of the conversation by impenetrable local references and thinks, "The whole town is like this. A cult."

He's right, I think; there is a cult here, and Keillor is perceptive enough to make note of it, however obliquely, but too much indebted to it to push past its surface. He is both its creator and its custodian. His wit and his indefatigable charm act as buffers between a surface of nostalgic delights and what might lie behind them. Late in the book, Johnny Tollefson comes back from a successful first year at St. Cloud State College intent on becoming a writer. He makes a list of the three things he needs to be a real writer. Number one, unwritten for his mother's sake, is sex; number two is Europe; and number three is despair. With little chance at hand for one or two, he goes to the Sidetrack Tap in search of number three. He doesn't find it. "The Sidetrack wasn't much as despair goes," says Keillor, "but it was convenient." This is charm and gentle wit getting in the way of honesty. Johnny might not find the despair he's after because he's not at all certain what it is he wants, but after more than 300 pages Keillor, we could argue, owes us a little candor. The depressions of swank bars are hedged by conspicuous swank; the desolations of strange, bustling places are mitigated by the expectation of variety. The desperation of small-town bars, like that of neighborhood taverns, is deepened by the weight of the familiar and darkened by the improbability of change.

For all its detail, the Sidetrack Tap is not real; it was never meant to be. Like the Chatterbox Café and Ralph's Pretty Good Grocery, it is a stage for foibles, those telling little errors that define Lake Wobegon in general. The drift everywhere is toward Norman Rockwell. Take a character from *Winesburg, Ohio*, which first appeared in 1919 in an age far less exacting in its psychological investigations than our own—Alice Hinman, for example, the clerk in the dry-goods store, who is so overcome by passionate restlessness that she runs naked into a rainstorm looking for anyone to embrace, waiting for the rain on her skin to transform and satisfy her—transpose her to Lake Wobegon, and she would stand out like an Edvard Munch figure in one of Rockwell's *Saturday Evening Post* covers.

Perhaps I am asking more than I should of a book that began as an entertainment on a Saturday-night radio program, which is itself a nostalgic reconstruction of old-fashioned local radio shows. The problem with Garrison Keillor is that he knows more than he's telling or more than he can afford to tell. There are two endings to *Lake Wobegon Days*. In the first, an anonymous young man is leaving the town, perhaps, given his deliberation and speed, for good. In the second, another man drives to the Sidetrack Tap in a blizzard for a pack of cigarettes. On the way home the snow is so thick that he can't see through the windshield. Instead, he leans down out of the opened door to follow the tracks in the road. As his car slides into a ditch, he realizes that he has been following the track of his own front tire and not the road at all. The slide into the ditch is a gentle one; his house, "where people love him and will be happy to see his face," is not far off. The accident that put him in the ditch is pure Lake Wobegon, a telling error of no great consequence. The first of these endings is the one that is characteristic of the end of America's small towns, the end my friend in that old pickup truck predicted. Everyone but the old and infirm leaves. The second is Keillor's testimony of affection—clever, charming, and consolingly false.

# 8

## You Are What You Drive

In the model for America's industrial future being circulated by
Reagan-era optimists, the smokestack industries, including the
automobile industry, will wither away and be replaced by a High
Tech industrialism that is clean, safe, and economically secure. No
more "dark satanic mills" and no more blue-color labor force. High
Tech exporting industries will be situated in proliferating Silicon
Valleys that will look like the office complexes that sprout up near
shopping malls, with circular driveways, chromium corporate
logos, and decorative fountains—"all watched over by machines of
loving grace." It's an attractive vision, I suppose, a future worth
believing in for an age that has reason enough to doubt the future
altogether. If it all sounds a bit too convenient, an apology over-
grown into a utopia—that's the way it is with panaceas. Still,
mourning the loss, for whatever reason, of industrial pollution,
clamoring assembly lines, energy depletion, and urban blight would
be crazy. But there is another loss predicted here, or rather the final
stages of a loss we already feel. There is no place in this vision for
the American car, at least not in the form we know and, with some
embarrassment, love. The American car, that crooked mirror to all
our whims, was the personalized, final product of the old industrialism at its dizziest and most euphoric heights, a tribute to excess,

even wretched excess, and so, in the American way of things, a mark of our success.

The importance of cars to the evolution of American life in this century is incalculable. The automotive industry has been central to the American economy for decades. Its executives and, with them, its modes of thought have moved freely into government since the 1930s. Detroit thinking has had a significant role in American domestic and foreign policy since the Depression. Remember, "What's good for General Motors is good for the U.S.A." The automobile shaped our cities to its own needs, then very nearly abandoned them; and the interstate highway system, a monument as spectacular in its own perverse way as the pyramids—larger and many times more costly—reshaped the American countryside.

The social impact of cars is even more staggering. The modern extended family, strung out from city neighborhoods to a succession of suburbs, is threaded together by cars. Courtship and marriage depend on them, and so, given the exigencies of joint custody, does divorce. Cars are the implements not only of our exaggerated love of mobility, but the only available means of coping with our fragmentations—the fragmentations of community and family and the fragmentations of the self, as well. Cars are instruments of identity. *You are what you drive.* Or *were*, since the oil crisis and Detroit's slow reaction to it have brought the future of the industry into question and put extreme limitations on the shapes of cars themselves and on their fun-house renditions of our psyches.

If we cannot have extravagant cars in the old mode, we can, at least, be extravagant in our nostalgia. Leon Mandel's *American Cars* is a large, lavishly produced book full of beautiful color photographs. In size and weight it is a coffee-table book, something for collectors and enthusiasts, and it would be easy to dismiss it on those grounds, but the text is substantial, informative, and entertaining, and, even more surprising for a book in this format, it is argumentative. Mandel has been a senior editor with both *Motor Trend* and *Car and Driver*, and so is a practiced hand at automobile prose, that breezy combination of technical data, physical description, and behind-the-wheel sensuality. For each of the historic periods he treats, Mandel offers a view of society in general and of the automotive industry's place in it. This is followed by a section on technological developments, which treats the evolutions of individual cars. Finally, and most engagingly, there is a section that attempts to give the reader a feel for the driving characteristics of a typical car of the period. Here Mandel tries to create a feel for the driver as well as the car. Spins are taken in a 1904 Olds Runabout, a Model T Ford, a 1929 Chevrolet, a 1929 Duesenberg SJ, a 1949 Ford, a Plymouth Roadrunner, and a Javelin. In the book's last drive, a 1955 Chevy owner is transported into the driver's seat of a GM X-car, a new Buick Skylark—an impressive ending because the '55 Chevy is so much a part of our sense of the best of the postwar era in cars.

The history of American cars is inevitably a history of car builders, and Mandel includes incidental biographies of some of the industry's moguls and madcap entrepreneurs in each of the early periods. Since the fifties the business of building automobiles has been dominated by executives and by what Mandel disdainfully calls accountants, profit-and-loss experts who have come to control design, engineering, and marketing. The drift, of course, was always away from a designer-owner (Fred Duesenberg or E. L. Cord) to a manager-strategist like Alfred Sloan of GM, whose chief innovations were the annual model change and the line-and-staff corporate organization. The industry, in its fledgling period, attracted innovators, craftsmen, and industrial adventurers. A good deal of this risky business was foreclosed by the Depression and the war, but in the postwar period a few fliers were taken—the Tucker, the Muntz, the Henry J, the Cunningham, and the Crosley—none of which succeeded. The Big Three (Ford, GM, and Chrysler) had an absolute hold on the market, and the last stages of Mandel's treatment of the industry is a chronicle of cynicism and institutionalized arrogance. Trends were created to lure buyers. Innovations were created in advertising meetings. Engines and transmissions for standard showroom models were tailored to the suicidal impulses of late-night street racers. Detroit had spent years avoiding the question of safety and so had contributed to the carnage by neglect or in the name of economy, but with the muscle cars of the late sixties, designed to capture the youth market, it became a deliberate accomplice. The measured skid mark and the head print in the windshield were part of the design, a no-cost extra in the "performance package."

For all of its expertise and its road-test acuity, the text of *American Cars* easily subsides to the photographs. If the car is, as Mandel claims, "the central artifact of our national life," these photographs are a patriotic homage. Some of the pictures are simply documentary in approach, but others have a reverence about them and a loving attention to detail. There is a photo essay on wooden spoked wheels, another on hood ornaments, and another on emblems. The classics—Duesenbergs, Pierce Arrows, and Cords—are represented with long views down their hoods or ground-level shots of their grills that make them seem like the architectural monuments they originally imitated. There is a Duesenberg Town Car that looks as though its coach work were made of draped satin—a platinum gray furl of metal, each line softened into a lengthening curve from its teardrop headlights to its skirted rear wheels. These classics reflect their own kind of excess; custom-made for the most part, with huge engines and every conceivable engineering device, including servo-assisted brakes and speedometer-actuated chassis lubrication, they were made for luxury and speed.

It is impossible to browse through these pictures and not be

caught up in one or another kind of nostalgia. My grandfather had
an Essex and a Packard sedan; one of my uncles had a Hupmobile,
and another changed my entire life at summer camp when he
brought my mother to visit in his 1940 Lincoln-Zephyr Continen-
tal, its oversize whitewalls spewing crushed rock and its V-12
engine rumbling with an authority borrowed from the gods. How
he managed to own the car is still a mystery since he was never
regularly employed. He simply owned cars. He could have just as
easily turned up in a DeSoto with metal-lidded headlights or a
Studebaker President. The Zephyr, one of the last attempts at a car
in the classic mode, was awesome, and the fascists who ran the
camp treated me with deference from that day on, as though the
ax-blade grill of the car somehow hovered over them on my behalf.
The '48 Plymouth I had in high school is here, and though my '49
Olds is not pictured, its engine is described.

In the early 1950s a broad knowledge of cars was a prerequisite
for a reasonable fantasy life—cars you wanted, cars that were
beneath contempt, driving characteristics, top speeds, transmissions. The detail was sometimes accurate but more often just
legendary, part of an oral tradition that moved daily from kid to
kid. On summer afternoons we would sit up on a retaining wall and
call out the names of passing cars with a desperation toward a
perfect score that rivaled anything anyone did in school. If dates
were a part of the game there were heated arguments, but since the
cars we were quarreling over were long gone, the disagreements
were resolved by passion and obscenity. Everyone claimed to be
able to drive. These were the early stages of the identification of car
with self. By the mid-fifties, when Detroit was devoting itself to
hype, it made the phony secrecy of new models and the arc lights
and ballyhoo of first showings seem reasonable. It carried us
through tail fins, portholes, and push-button automatic transmissions and laid the groundwork for Detroit's play of names, in which

PART TWO

the car you bought defined your resources while its model name
whispered your aspirations: Bel Air for citizens of Berwyn or
Biscayne for Tinley Park; Grand Prix and Le Mans for even more
distant dreamers; for the fearless a menagerie of wild animals—
Mustang, Cougar, Wildcat, Barracuda—or an array of weapons—
Cutlass, Javelin, F-86 (after the Korean War jet fighter); and for the
ultimate fantasist an old dream with front-wheel drive, El Dorado.
It is a good measure of the automobile's fall from mythic grace that
we now buy cars called Brat and Scamp and Rabbit.

On the practical side of things, the game of car has only one
rule—you lose. The point of play is to see how gracefully or with
what vehemence you do so. Road handling, for example, is a good
counter to your car's failure to start on cold mornings. It's illusive
and idiosyncratic enough to evade argument, and it makes you
seem so much more discriminating than people whose cars merely
run. Craftsmanship, despite the rising tide of rust, is an answer to
age. Complexity, in the curious world of auto-psyche, seems a
reasonable excuse for frequent mechanical breakdowns, especially if
you remind the passing critic or your next-door neighbor that the
unassailable Ferrari can't be driven across the country unless it is
closely followed by a trained mechanic driving a van full of tools
and spare parts. If all else fails, you can always retreat behind the
great deal you made, those few hard-nosed minutes you spent in the
thinly partitioned office at the dealership that left the salesman
weeping at the financial loss suffered at your hands. The car has
been our primer in the failure of made things, a course in planned
obsolescence and decay taught near the center of dreams.

The trade is movement and its illusion of freedom. And sometimes it works. The lake slips by; roadside trees reel past you like
clouds; curves sweep; and the traffic parts. The teasing illegalities of
speed seem as inevitable as original sin, and out there, just beyond
the edge of sight, lurks the accident that finally defines the experi-

68

ence and gives it shape, the statistical gamble we play at each day and reward television and movies, with their high-speed chases, for exaggerating each night. If the car, gleaming as it does in all the pictures in Mandel's book, is the central artifact of American life, it has a double—the mangled wreck, the persistent, alternative destination that is never seen in these pages: 50,000 dead each year, another four million injured. The dream the car serves must be a powerful one to tolerate such destruction. It's hard to imagine its place being taken by video games and home computers, however pleasant the result of such an exchange might promise to be.

# 9

## Starting

"First of all, I pat the gas, just once, with the key off. Then I turn the key on, push it all the way to the floor, and let up slowly. Halfway up and I start it."

"With mine, you gotta hold the pedal all the way down to the floor, crank it till it catches, and when it does, let it up about two-thirds of the way."

Five or six of us are stamping around the outer lobby of my apartment building in down parkas and ski gloves. It is January in Chicago, one of the mornings of the car. Outside, the bright sun gives the air a blue sheen like finely worked carbon steel. It scrapes against the glass front wall of the lobby and hones itself along the three-week mounds of snow layered like limestone beside the walk.

"Four times." It's Eddie leaning against the heater vents behind the mailboxes. His tone is canonical. "Four times. Just pump it four times, and it starts right up."

"I try to go out at night, you know, and start her up. And after the engine's hot, I rev it up real high, turn the key off, and push the gas all the way down. You can just hear her sucking gas up to the engine."

"Well, with my diesel, you have to wait for this light on the dash to go off. That means the glow plug's hot enough to start it, but by then on a day like today, you've used up too much of the battery, and it won't start anyway."

Diesel? Light on the dash? No wonder his car doesn't start. Cars that start have a system, a private ritual worked out by their owners on days like this one, sitting shivering and hopeful in their machines. They have, these devices, the force of private truth—how and when and how many times the pedal is pushed, how far the choke is pulled out and when, whether the key is turned on before or after the pedal is pushed. Some of this lore comes from tow-truck jump starters who bob up from under the hood and shout, "Keep it all the way to the floor," or "Get your foot off the gas," or "Pump it." How much of this really matters is impossible to know. It matters, obviously, to the way we live with cars, and standing around the lobby with the guys it has a curiously familiar and disquieting ring to it, a touch of early high-school locker-room sex education—vain, improbable, idiosyncratic, and just as indispensable.

There is something intimate, however painful, about trying to start your car on a bitter cold morning. After the little rituals of pedal pushing and precision choke pulling, the deepening, sad song of a slowing starter motor, the inside of the windshield hazed over with your own quickening breath, a haze eventually webbed with threads of self-propelled crystal that run at loony angles across the glass. Bits of advice, a lifetime of pseudomechanic's lore carols up out of the collective technological unconscious—to avoid flooding the engine put the gas pedal to the floor, or to avoid flooding the engine keep your foot off the pedal entirely, pump it, never pump it, add heat, crank it, don't crank it you'll wear down the battery, try it again, call the motor club.

The engine is nearing death, and the starter's grind reaches a slow, trembling note that is as much attuned to sadness and despair as the loneliest of Big Walter Horton's quavering train-whistle obbligatos or the most mournful of B. B. King's spine-quivering chords. By now you're bowing into the steering wheel, your stomach tightening as the engine slows, the edge of the cold key cutting into your finger and your thumb. You try each contradictory piece of advice in turn—first slowly, punctuating each separate attempt with a moment of silence, then rapidly, in quick succession, until the dashboard warning lights darken and the last bit of energy from the overburdened battery clicks like ice on glass against the failing solenoid.

This is the zero point of your love of your car, your love of cars in general, the moral retribution for every sin it has suffered on your account, punishment for a long string of specific failures beginning with the profligacies of the show room and ending with last night's lack of concern for a full gas tank and for an even longer misguided faith in the efficacy of cars, all the way back to the first moment in late childhood when you knew, watching a Pontiac Catalina drift by like a cream-and-turquoise Beatrice, that wheels were the way to freedom, love, and happiness. Neighbors slip by on the way to work. Old Chevys clamor to life, rust-bitten Fords, the painfully modest compact in the next parking stall, all of them kicking up white plumes of exhaust above the blackening snow. Just one rebuke after another.

*Mea culpa, mea culpa, mea maxima culpa . . .* or hit the steering wheel in disgust . . . or stand outside in the cold, the hood up and your battery cables raised like a begging bowl. At 26 below help comes from all sides. Everyone's tragedy is no one's tragedy. But at a mere ten below, you are alone, a very special and conspicuous failure, leprous, unclean.

Nothing, except love and America, promises more than a car, so there are few disappointments more bitter. Remember when you saw it on television, swooning like a dancer through the curves of a mountain road as lushly green as any of the emerald visions of the

73

Hudson River school or skimming the surface of Pacific Ocean water along the California coast or conquering the Baja or lasering toward the vanishing point of a crayon-colored Mojave sunset, irresistibly lustrous and fluid? They don't sell us cars with tires whitened with salt and salt streaks trailing like tears from the lash tips of their windshield wipers, this Lot's wife of a car, immovable, dead.

10

## Be Your Own Best Friend

A current television commercial shows Danny Kaye and a group of children watching a small-screen movie of themselves at a birthday party that obviously has occurred just moments before. The product being advertised is Polavision, an at-home instant-replay device. After a brief explanation of the product, Kaye looks out at the television audience and says, "If you don't have Polavision, there's something missing from your life." It is not merely that we are missing a photo-mechanical novelty, but that something crucial is missing from the rich, full life we all deserve. By itself, the remark would be bizarre, even outrageous. The machine being sold here just records—and only within a limited range of a life's activity. In contemporary American culture, though, the need for images of ourselves has become so great that this sales pitch hardly seems extraordinary. We use photographs to record our existence, in some ways to verify it. We take more pictures of ourselves than of the things around us, and each of us carries through life albums or shoe boxes full of pictures that validate family, friends, child-hood, marriage, and nativity. Instant pictures—Polaroids and their counterparts—are more mirrorlike for giving us back ourselves and our surroundings not as they were but as they are. And Polavision is, clearly, another part of the arsenal of self-verification. In a life sustained by images, cameras and other recording devices take on a primary, active role, investing events with reality.

The Polavision commercial is a model for one kind of contemporary narcissism—an adult and children viewing themselves in domestic celebration while the bits and pieces of that celebration still lie scattered around them. Obviously, the party was interrupted for this viewing of the party. The image event overpowers the real event while we look on through that most intricate of contemporary looking-glasses, the television screen, at carefully contrived versions of ourselves, whose actions we struggle to keep pace with. The mythological Narcissus died for the love of his own image in a clear pool; contemporary narcissism has an entire technology at its disposal and, according to Christopher Lasch, a general culture more and more adapted to its needs.

Lasch is an American historian who has written in the past on radicalism and on the American Left, and *The Culture of Narcissism* is clearly the work of a historian. Lasch's argument, that contemporary culture is best characterized with reference to narcissism, as configured by the myth and as more complexly drawn by psychiatric accounts of clinical narcissism, is in its broadest terms unassailable. It is possible to quibble here and there with various parts of the analysis, but the metaphor sweeps so much of contemporary life up so handily that for much of the book it is easier to add to his examples than to doubt them.

Aside from obvious instances of mirroring, such as the Polavision commercial, narcissism involves other forms of self-absorption. Lasch's treatment of the therapeutic manias in contemporary culture is especially persuasive. We are awash in panaceas based on self-awareness and self-help, from encounter groups to sex clinics. Even the current passion for athletics has its quasi-mystical, narcissistic side—*Running and Being*, as one of the joggers' most rhapsodic texts has it.

Because encounter groups are social organizations devised for narcissistic purposes, they suggest the direction in which the "culture of narcissism" is moving American society. For most of human history, social contracts have required an exchange of individual liberty for the advantages of the group. By contrast, the encounter group is convened primarily to witness the unfolding self of the individual member. Instead of offering custom and stability, it is transient and incidental by design. Much of our political history has been involved with the contract between individuals and the state, redefining both liberties and obligations. In a society extrapolated from the encounter group, politics can be only another form of personal exposition, a spectacle of self in which power means the ability to corral an audience. Celebrity becomes not the by-product of political activity but its goal, and the activity itself becomes increasingly desperate. Arthur Bremmer, George Wallace's attacker, wrote in his diary that an assassination (and it didn't seem to matter whom he killed) would get him on the Johnny Carson or Dick Cavett show. In his treatment of the New Left, Lasch presents a fair range of examples of the self-absorption that has invaded politics in America; he also deals with narcissistic traits of such mainstream political figures as Kennedy, Johnson, and Nixon.

Perhaps the most striking sections in the book, however, are those that examine contemporary corporate life. Using both sociological studies of management behavior and popular self-help texts for executives, Lasch evolves a picture of corporate and bureaucratic life that fits remarkably well with current descriptions of pathological narcissism. The new-style corporate manager plays a game in which the positive characteristics are mobility, style, panache, and "a winning image." Matters of substance have very little to do with success, and the intense loyalties of the "organization man" are obsolete and dysfunctional. One of the most extreme of the recent get-ahead books even included a list of "winner" and "loser" products that went so far as to name brands of shoes that could mark a corporate loser. The force of Lasch's presentation comes from the agreement he finds between this kind of popular material and academic studies.

Narcissism, in Lasch's view, pervades all of contemporary life. Not only does it remove achievement as a goal in business, but it degrades, as well, the rituals of play. With their arbitrary but essential rules, games provide settings for the ritual enactment of aggression, skill, and strategy. Sports become trivial when athletic performance is too involved with celebrity or when mere participation on the playground is a goal in itself. Lasch's critique of contemporary sports is a novel one because it avoids the antiprofessionalism of the standard liberal criticism and the anticombative argument of the New Left. For Lasch, sports serve us best as shared illusions in which rules and the conventions of play focus and absorb our attention. Narcissitic self-involvement fragments the illusion, and the fragile social structure is shattered into a loose array of mirrors, like so much broken glass in a vacant lot.

Lasch finds a similar decline in our ability to share other illusions, such as the conventions of fiction and theatre. Much of the experimentation of contemporary novelists and playwrights is seen as narcissistic. Novels that intentionally collapse their own verisimilitude with flights of self-consciousness about writing and theatres that work at breaking across the boundaries of the stage are included here. Yet the most extreme of these experiments seem to me to proceed not out of a lack of faith in illusion, as Lasch has it, but rather from a conviction that certain artistic conventions are too firmly implanted in the audience, to the point of being entirely confused with reality. Still, Lasch's argument that all of this proceeds from a failure of aesthetic contracts is a solid one.

*The Culture of Narcissism* includes lengthy discussions of family life and contemporary sexuality. One of the recurrent themes of these and other discussions is what Lasch calls "The war of all against all." The narcissist, deeply dependent on others for reflective approbation, is also fearful of dependencies and extended relationships. With its usual grotesque accuracy, popular culture now defines success as the acquisition of enough power to enforce the whims of self-involvement on others, an authority it confers on Greek tycoons, conglomerate heads, and Mafia chieftans.

Lasch's analysis is exhaustive, but it is well worth following to the end. Even though the thesis seems proven at the outset, the book's treatment of historical backgrounds and contemporary trends is persuasive, if a little frightening, throughout.

# 11

## The Ties That Bind

Choosing a tie is like choosing what you want to say, but it is a choice you make in advance—in the morning, with the whole day in mind, or in the evening, with the night's promises like pools of light in the distance. It is a chance to predict what is going to happen. All the earlier steps are just dressing; when you sort through a tie rack, pull out the one that seems to suit what lies ahead, and test it with one or two pulls against the back of your upturned collar, you are being arrayed. There ought to be music, heralds perhaps or a Spanish trumpet from *Blood and Sand* or *Death in the Afternoon*.

My father has a place in this ritual. He sits off to the side, a quiet witness, in his darkest suit, his own broad, flat tie done up in a simple four-in-hand, the straight-forward kind of knot that Jimmy Stewart used in *It's a Wonderful Life* and *Mr. Smith Goes to Washington*. I prefer the substance and contour of ties with double linings and the inverted near-pyramid of a half-Windsor knot, a baroque turn of phrase he would have disapprovingly associated with the likes of Adolphe Menjou and Claude Rains. The knot reminds me of the colossal full Windsors we used on charcoal-gray knit ties in the 1950s under the pink flying buttresses of a Mr. B collar, so I draw it up to my neck with a certain residual delinquency. When you choose a tie, you choose a version of yourself—part father, part friends, part banker, part mountebank—to take into the world. Setting some ties aside because they are worn or soiled or just out of fashion is a sorrowful business. It's like giving up on aeronautics, deep-sea diving, or polar exploration, something else to add to the growing catalogue of loss.

For me, a necktie is the last surviving token of the brocade jacket, the velvet waistcoat, silk stockings, powdered wigs, cross garters, spats, lace cuffs, and the jewel-studded walking stick, all the plumes and gilt of the court or the promenade commemorated in a narrow strip of silk. Before the Victorian age, finery was the essential stuff of public man. Ties are more modest, certainly, but they are public in the same way. You wear a tie expecting to be seen. Ties may be the only remaining sign of expecting to be seen; and being seen, not just noticed but seen, is something to be cherished in a world in which so much escapes attention.

I worry a little that this has grown too serious, but I have frequently been accused of being too serious about ties, either directly or by sneering implication—as in "You wore a tie" or "Another tie?" I wore ties while the rest of the world drifted toward flowered shirts and buckskin, wore them straight through the days of the dress turtleneck and love beads. Earnest strangers with the divine right of waning parties told me that my ties were indications of aggression, repression, materialism, decadence, and political and social revisionism. A girl in a bar on Hubbard Street once held my tie—a wool Polo with swirling red figures—gently with both hands while her boyfriend threatened to break my neck.

As with so many other extremely personal matters, men tend not to talk about their ties. They buy them, wear them, and occasionally acknowledge the other ties around them, but it's very rare to find men who can sit down and talk through the real issues involved in neckties. When a tie wholesaler at the Merchandise Mart showed

me through the mad variety of this season's neckties, he said that
there was probably a support group in a Chicago suburb for men
with tie problems. I began calling around trying to find a group I
could sit in on. The more I searched for it the more plausible the
group became.

It was late fall. I put the handwritten instructions on the seat beside
me and headed for Oak Park—west on the chewed and battered
Eisenhower to Harlem, Harlem north to Erie, east on Erie. The
group met in the music room of a landmark house—six drawing-
room chairs around a large coffee table, a tea service already set out,
and a boxworth of Pepperidge Farm butter cookies. I have never
really felt at ease with *support* or *encounter* or *mutual help* groups,
those wayward, temporary societies in which confession is the
currency of attention. This one, which sat so close to one of my
own totems, made me particularly anxious.

I had spent an hour choosing a tie for the occasion. These were
aficionados, after all, not the usual "Mmm, nice tie" crowd, but
devotees. I tried an old Polo wool with oversize paisley in dark blue
and cream on purple, not the one in the bar but a close cousin. It
seemed too much, too declarative for a subtle audience, out of scale,
like a soccer move on a chess board. Perhaps, I thought, the French
diagonal wool plaid, navy and deep lavender on red—it seemed to
go in the right direction, a slightly satiric variation on a somewhat
somber theme. Or a Liberty, the diagonal patchwork in wool
challis, all the colors muted, but each pattern lush and consequential
to the next. Why woolens? It wasn't just the season. Audacity in
wool comes harder than in silk. But, then, for a subtle audience, a
very subtle remark in silk, an aside, might mean even more. So
silks. Nothing obvious or easy, no simple gaud would do. I passed
over the obvious, considered but discarded regimental stripes in
discordant colors as somewhat snide, and settled on a soft-mauve

paisley, muted to the point of vanishing, with silver-gray outlining in the print. Just right, a lush, restrained, classic pattern, varied in the direction of soft monochrome.

Larry, the group leader—a Rogerian psychologist, I had been told—met me at the door to the house. He wore a blue button-down oxford-cloth shirt, open at the neck. I was not surprised. Of course, the shrink would take a neutral stance with a hint of superiority. The shirt was J. Press. It could, he was saying, take a tie with ease. We chatted in the archway between the foyer and the music room. The group had been together for about a year, he told me. It was one of several groups he conducted. Equally specialized? I asked. It depends on your point of view, he answered with a professional lilt.

The group's regular members arrived, shed their coats in the hall, and moved efficiently into the music room. Larry left to get hot water for the tea. There wasn't a tie in the group, not one. There wasn't even a regular shirt. Art, the stockbroker, wore a New Zealand rugby shirt. Dave, the maître d', had on one of those California casuals in soft cotton that had no collar at all. Forrest, the lawyer, and John, the endocrinologist, both had turtlenecks. I felt betrayed; all that time choosing the right tie had been wasted. Not only were they not wearing ties; they were paying no attention to mine. I began to feel as though I had committed an unpardonable error like a guy with a pitcher of stingers at an AA meeting. I crossed my arms over my chest and settled in. Larry was back, fidgeting over the tea tray. He took his chair and said, "Who wants to start?"

There's no point in telling you what I expected. This was a support group for tie addicts. You know what I expected: tales of family and business collapse caused by ties; the previous week's temptations, foulards glimpsed and envied at the office; a new display in a shop window on La Salle Street, ties radiant as Apollo's hair around a poker hand of dress shirts; that small display I always hesitate over at the Water Tower, right next to the escalator, pastel cottons with comic-book hot dogs, hamburgers, and ice-cream cones stitched on; gnawing desires for the feel of double linings, the plain, interior silk enveloping a coarse muslin frame; hankerings after the unfashionable width of broad rapacious ties; gangster yearnings for grotesque prints over dark shirts. But there was none of that. Perhaps all of the detail had been confessed out of them; perhaps it was never there.

Art talked first and was entirely concerned with buttons—shirt buttons, the buttons on his vest, how often he buttoned or rebuttoned his coat and his vest in the course of the day, the tie covering his shirt buttons, the vest covering his tie with its own regimen of buttons, and the large, presiding button on his suit coat. Dave said that Art was overconcerned with hierarchy, and Larry asked if anyone wanted to go with that. Forrest said that all of his ties, 226 of them, were all the same, so he wasn't the least bit hierarchical. Larry asked if sameness wasn't a more extreme form of hierarchy because arbitrary choice is an amulet of power. John said that he was still working on his anxiety over the two points of his ties. Apparently John was nervous to the point of obsession about getting the underside of his tie within a quarter of an inch of the top. Dave said let it all hang out, and everyone laughed. It was the only hint of the phallic tie in the hour we were there. I waited for Larry to say, "Does anyone want to go with that?" and remembered the burlesque sketch where the comic's tie pops up whenever the strip-teaser, dressed in a scanty nurse's uniform, torches by, but Larry bustled at the tea and offered me a cookie. No Priapus in Oak Park, I guess.

It went on. The tea cooled and the butter cookies disappeared. Art recognized his father in the buttonings and himself in the unbuttonings. Larry smiled like a carpenter over a well-fitted joint.

Dave apologized for a hostility that I hadn't even noticed and said he guessed he had a long way to go. Forrest said he thought hostility was a sign of affection, and John said that most things even out in the end. As we were leaving, Larry said, "Well?" "Very interesting," I replied. I looked at the easy sincerity of Larry's opened collar, then down at my tie, all its subtlety unused and unappreciated, and let it say all that I could not about that evening, a few slashing remarks worthy of Cyrano.

In *The Language of Clothes* Alison Lurie says not only that clothes speak but also that they have a grammar and syntax of their own. She even suggests that different pieces of clothing may function as different parts of speech. Her notion is that accessories are adjectives and adverbs. That's all well and good for circle pins and smart little scarves, but ties are only modifiers in the lingo of clothing salesmen. In a good men's store the salesman brings a handful of ties to your new suit and lays them across the lapel one at a time in a ceremony of staid, editorial revision. The goal is always harmony, the compatible, already implicit adjective; so the leitmotif of the suit can be the theme of the tie, but tone is always maintained with a consistency of brightness and hue. He doesn't bring you ties that will make the suit seem dull, listless or inconsequential—no brash adjectives or hip disclaimers for their sedate, costly nouns. It is this process, neoclassical in its aversion to contrast, that has filled the world with dull, politic ties, modest adjectival squires to nice suits.

In use ties function quite differently, not so much as modifiers but as interjections, as in "Hey" or more firmly, in conversational Chicago, "Eh!" In polite circumstances a paisley or an English floral is more likely to say "Well" or "Hmm." Not all ties are abrupt. Some behave more like conjunctions: the sedately matched tie with its purely functional "and"; the slightly unexpected, not yet audacious, "but"; or the curiously unsettled and unsettling "or." There are even more specialized functions, like Studs Terkel's red knit "neither," its disquieting half syntax completed by his checked shirt's obligatory "nor." Extraordinary gestures made in special settings sometimes act like demonstratives—the bow tie in the courtroom, saying "this" and, by obvious, devastating contrast, "that."

We wear ties in situations in which we are expected to act like grownups. To some extent, that means that we are preparing for situations in which we cannot say all that we want to say or do all that we might like to do. Ties let us add a rejoinder or a disclaimer. When ties are particularly garish, they are loud. The pleasure of neckties is that you add the disclaimer or the exclamation with the same article of clothing you use to suggest that you are above such things.

# III

PART THREE

12

# Of Living Belfry and Rampart:

## On American Literary Magazines Since 1950

**1**

A number of years ago the editor of *Young Guard*, the principal literary magazine for Soviet writers under forty, visited my office in Chicago. He and several companions were touring the United States west to east—Hollywood, Disneyland, the Grand Canyon, a Kansas wheatfield, an Iowa cornfield, Chicago's Michigan Avenue, and, by sheer social accident, the Swallow Press: a dusty, chaotic loft, half a block from police headquarters, south of the Loop in the natural habitat of marginal commerce and the half-pint bottle. We drank coffee, exchanged cigarettes, and through a translator talked about literature and publishing. We toured the offices and the warehouse. It must have been a strange experience for the Soviet editor—that gaping old structure, with wooden beams exposed above pallets of unsold poetry books, the busy disarray of the offices, the blare of WVON Soul Radio from the packing table in the back room, classical FM in stereo from atop the file cabinets in the office space in front, the regular thud of falling objects in the Senior Citizens' Workshop one floor up. State Department tours do not, as a matter of course, feature sight-seeing at the raffish edges of capitalism. I couldn't tell whether he thought we were dilettantes or lunatics, but it was clear that our experience had very little in common with his. Back in my office, he browsed through the shelves of literary magazines on the wall beside my desk. "What are these things?" he asked, holding an early copy of *Toothpick, Lisbon and the Orcas Islands* until the translator finished the question in English.

"Literary magazines."

The answer made its way to him in Russian. He glanced at the shelves again, then at his companion, an agricultural economist in amber-tinted glasses, and asked that the answer be repeated. The shelves held three or four years' worth of fifty or so literary magazines. "How can there be so many?" I explained that what I had was barely a sample of the number of magazines being produced across the country. Again he questioned the translator about my answer. "And do they all have many readers?" I told him that some had very few readers. "How many?" He was doing arithmetic in his head, trying to figure the enormity of a literature that could sustain all this, I suppose. His magazine in Russia had a circulation of more than 200,000, with regional and ethnic supplements. It was the point of entry for most young writers into the writers' union, and so was essential to employment. It was also the key to publication by the magazine's book publishing affiliate.

"A few—just two or three—have circulations of about 10,000," I said. "Most are printed in runs of less than 2,000 copies, and many have fewer than a hundred readers." The translation reached him like a cool breeze, and he relaxed a bit. If this was to be the day on which the literature gap was discovered, at least he would be on the high side. He was still puzzled. What was the point of having so many magazines with so few readers? Wouldn't it be better to have just a few magazines that everyone interested in literature could read?

He pulled more magazines down from the shelf: an *Antioch Review*, thick as an anthropology textbook in paperback; *Kayak,* bantamweight in rough paper with untrimmed edges, on the cover an old engraving demonstrating the use of an antique prosthetic device; a yellowed *Floating Bear* in uncertain mimeograph; *Extensions*, deliberately international and tidy as a French suitcoat; a more ample *Chicago Review* with a busy post-psychedelic drawing of a tree on the cover; *Goliards* in high-gloss newsstand format and disjointed graphics, like a top hat decked out with fishing flies and campaign buttons; *Poetry*, as thin, sedate, and costly as a dowager empress. There was a last question—unasked, perhaps unformulated. He shuffled through the pile of magazines he had moved to my desk, confused and a little embarrassed. I tried hard to explain the kind of diversity the magazines represented and said something, oft-repeated during years of fund-raising, about their place in the history of modern literature. The translator worked away at this like a tireless journeyman with a bad set of blueprints and knotted lumber. The Russian listened, trying to arrange the magazines at hand into a pile that would not fall over. I wanted to convey something of a romance of little magazines, their individuality and the deep personal commitments that sustain them—something, that is, of my own attachment to them. My interrogator nodded at the translator's version of my flourish, but without conviction. He was acquiescing, not agreeing.

I consoled myself with the notion that in riffling through those magazines in a disheveled Chicago editorial office he had seen more of American literary publishing than most literary visitors, and I confess to a certain perverse pride in the irregularity of it all—the odd idiosyncrasies of magazines so intent on individuality that they refuse to share a format that will make a neat stack or an orderly shelf. But where I saw freedom (or, at least, license), he saw ineffectual diffusion, yet another Disneyland where the illusion of choice is the disguise of limitation and fidgeting activity replaces movement. His questions were clearly rooted in Soviet literary and political bureaucracy, but they are not easily dismissed. *Why are there so many magazines? Who reads them, anyway? Wouldn't it be better to have fewer magazines with larger resources and more readers?* I have heard the same questions asked by U.S. government officials, foundation executives, and little magazine editors.

> Go in for scribenery with a satiety of arthurs . . . malady of milady made melodi of malodi.
>
> —James Joyce

**2**

In the introduction to *The Little Magazines: A History and a Bibliography*, authors Hoffman, Allen, and Ulrich estimated that six hundred little magazines had been published in English between 1912 and 1946. Informed guesswork—not much else is possible—suggests that at least fifteen hundred such magazines are being published in the United States right now. The figure is approximate because so many magazines exist so briefly. The Coordinating Council of Literary Magazines, a nonprofit organization that distributes state, federal, and private funds to magazines nationwide, has a current membership of over six hundred publications, and the organization requires that each member magazine must have published three issues and have existed for at least a year before applying for membership or financial support. *The Directory of Little Magazines and Small Presses* poses neither of these restrictions and offers a longer list, nearly a thousand; and it has to be assumed that magazines are published that do not find their way onto either list. A great number of magazines die before the appearance of a second issue. Three issues, the CCLM requirement, is a tough distance for most beginners. A modest first issue is likely to consume all the ready cash its editors can muster; with luck and a fair-sized circle of friends, donations and subscriptions can support a second number;

but the third issue has no natural resources. It is the one that naive editors suppose will be supported by sales, but it is a rule of literary magazine publishing that there are no sales, certainly none sufficient to sustain publication. Each year hundreds of magazines are born and die with one or two issues that never find their way onto lists or into copyright registry.

So the numbers are conjectural but extremely high—twice as many magazines in print at any moment in the mid-seventies as existed altogether in the first thirty-five years of little-magazine history. An explosion in little-magazine publication occurred in the late sixties and continues. It is supported in part by the availability of grants—from CCLM, state art councils, and the National Endowment for the Arts—but depends, as well, on a growing population of writers and on access to various kinds of printing technology. Nearly 67 percent of the magazines in CCLM's most recent catalogue (May 1977) have come into existence since 1970; less than 9 percent existed before 1960; and only eight magazines from Hoffman, Allen, and Ulrich's extensive bibliography survive. The world of little magazines is characterized not only by growth but by incessant change. Magazines die, not only because they lack funds but because their editors, often quite deliberately, allow them to die—sometimes out of frustration or exhaustion and sometimes because they feel that the task of the magazine has been accomplished. This last is especially true for magazines with a closely defined literary point of view and a tightly knit group of writers.

Little magazines have always functioned primarily for writers. Readers are desirable, sometimes even actively sought out, but the impulse behind most magazines is the writer-editor's conviction that there are writers who are not being served by existing publications. At their best, little magazines draw together groups of writers and, however marginally, find them an audience. In contrast, commercial magazines find audiences and financial support and then, almost incidentally, find their writers. Because of their attention to writers the little magazines register, in their numbers and shifting variety, the literary activity in the country. The modern quarterly emerged from a period of intense interest in criticism in the late thirties and forties and seemed to dominate the literary scene well into the fifties. Yet we see the fifties in retrospect as an intense period of activity, particularly in poetry, supported by a number of remarkable small magazines—*Ark, Contact, Folder, Circle, Measure, Poetry New York, Big Table*, the *Black Mountain Review*, and others—that deliberately set themselves against the larger magazines' reliance on criticism. More important, they had an entirely new group of writers to publish, among them Creeley, Duncan, Ginsberg, Merton, Olson, Levertov, Merwin, O'Hara, and Snyder. None of these magazines survive; of the "Chief Periodicals" listed by Donald Allen in *The New American Poetry, 1945–1960*, only two magazines are still publishing: *Poetry* and *Chicago Review*. The interplay between eclectic quarterlies and highly individualistic smaller magazines continued into the sixties; but the sharp line between critically buttressed work in quarterlies (once called *academic*) and newer work faded quickly as the numbers increased and as writers of all kinds found their way into expanded versions of academe.

In the sixties and seventies, the audience for serious literature has not grown nearly as fast as the number of writers. Some have claimed that the actual number of readers has diminished. Nonetheless, writers' workshops proliferate in colleges and universities (the final redoubts of failing English departments), and poets and fiction writers in increasing numbers enter the world in search of publication. For the first time in history, we may have more writers than readers. Editorial offices of established magazines are drifted over with manuscripts, and new magazines are born to meet the writers' needs for print. Increasingly, magazines seem to reflect a sociological circumstance as much as an aesthetic one.

Aesthetically most new magazines declare themselves to be avant-garde. Very few are. The declaration is ritualistic, a part of the magazine's acknowledgment of its lineage among the magazines of the first part of the century. Many of the recent magazines are really involved in the eccentric use of literary precedents—a useful procedure, but one that is more cautious and traditional than most editors would like to admit. Typically, a magazine will be generated out of a sense of common interest—even of immediate community— among writers. The editors write to one or two prominent figures they admire, asking for contributions. Sometimes, in less coherent groups, all that is being sought is a little authority with which to launch the project, that and some validation of the less notable writers the magazine will include. In more carefully organized groups, the figureheads define the magazine's aesthetic precedent. Thus the magazine's orbit is in perigee around its most notable contributor. Usually the writers chosen for these roles are not broadly accepted national figures—never a Lowell or a Berryman, Roth or Cheever—but are the distinguished vestiges of previous new waves. Modern American literature has seen a succession of avant-gardes; very few have captured an enduring authority. For all the ballyhoo, the center of American letters has remained fairly conservative since the 1930s.

An example of a magazine that started in this way is *Milk Quarterly*, a Chicago publication that emerged from a group of writers which met regularly. The magazine began as a forum for writing done by members of the group, but declared at the outset an allegiance to the New York School with regular appearances by Ted Berrigan. Berrigan gave precedent to much of what appeared in the magazine, though very little of what was published was directly generated from Berrigan's work. This kind of situation can be seen

in magazines with precedent-figures as different as Thomas Mc-
Grath, Thomas Lux, Charles Bukowski, Harold Norse, and Ed
Dorn. In the almost totally decentralized literature of the late sixties and early seventies, these associations are measures of what was
once called influence. Magazines of this sort can be seen as
developmental. What's going on is an experiment with the possibilities of a fairly well-articulated aesthetic; the play is outward
from, then back to, a source, like a game of hide-and-seek—furtive,
sometimes daring, but always in sight of home base. When the
exploration of possibilities is especially thorough or eccentric, the
magazine can be very exciting.

In their attachment to the very recent past (the day before
yesterday, in some cases), many magazines reflect a general trend in
the society; in America, after all, nostalgia has replaced history. The
association of literary movements with precedents is obviously not
new. The magazines that presented the "new poetry" of the 1950s
all exhibited strong ties to the modernists, to Pound and Williams
most firmly; they looked to a tradition of experimentation in the
twenties and before, and beyond that to Whitman. What is peculiar
to the contemporary use of literary precedent is that it is willing to
take its masters from so close at hand. With few exceptions, history,
at least literary history, is largely absent from newer magazines. In
addition to their role as adversaries to popular literary trends, the
magazines of the early part of the century exhibited a number of
broad historical and critical concerns. In *The Little Review, Dial,* and
*Hound and Horn* there appeared regularly essays by modern writers
that treated historical figures—reclamation, even conscription for
the movement of Dante, Homer, Blake, Shelley, the Elizabethans,
the Metaphysicals, the French. Ezra Pound's brief essay, "The
Tradition," first appeared in *Poetry* (III, 3, December 1913); essential
essays by Eliot and Joyce first appeared in *The Little Review* and *The
Dial,* along with essays by Santayana and Bertrand Russell. If the

modern movement was intent on reinventing the past to suit its own purposes, contemporary writing seems preoccupied with knitting up the tattered edges of the present. Few contemporary magazines take a critical stand; essays, even book reviews and correspondence, are less and less common, especially in newer magazines. Perhaps the weight of criticism that filled the quarterlies is still being counteracted, or it may be that the excesses of academic, scholarly criticism are now too apparent. There are exceptions. *Io*, which is involved primarily in myth and cosmology, is full of prose discourse by poets, but by design none of it is what would traditionally be called critical. At the other end of the scale is *Parnassus*, a magazine composed entirely of critical reviews of books of poetry. Some quarterlies still attempt a traditional balance of fiction, poetry, and criticism, but few of these have much critical authority among writers. *Partisan Review* sustains itself but with far less of the political and cultural focus it once had. *American Poetry Review* includes a great deal of commentary through a number of regular columns, and *Salmagundi* and *Massachusetts Review* are noteworthy for the consistently high quality of their critical essays. There are also some notable smaller magazines that have reserved space for closely focused commentary. *Kayak*, an exemplary smaller magazine in a number of ways, still includes letters and comments that have a clear relationship to the concerns of the magazine. Robert Bly's magazines (*The Fifties, The Sixties,* and *The Seventies*) have been models for idiosyncratic editing and highly personal critical commentary. Somewhere between the larger magazines with balanced content and these smaller, more personal publications is *Field*, a magazine with particular interests in translation and in surrealism, which has engaged a number of writers in important theoretical discussion.

There are broad literary differences among the magazines of the last three decades: university-based reviews with eclectic interests;

quarterlies with distinct critical frameworks; independent eclectic magazines that have invariably served the centrist literature nobly and well (*Poetry Northwest* and *Beloit Poetry Journal* are just two examples of this type of magazine); and adversary magazines, those quicksilver enterprises that hold much of the romance of the little magazines in their invariable insistence that everybody in print is wrong about nearly everything literary and cultural except the few people published in their thirty-two saddle-stitched, untrimmed pages. Distinctions among very recent magazines—the 69 percent founded since 1970—are less easily drawn. Obviously, the field is too big and too crowded. Differences are also confused by quarrels about size and funding. In the clamor for grants and the squabbling that has ensued, literary matters have been entangled with financial statements. "Hard-pressed" has been taken to include experimental; "independently owned" in some circles is synonymous with avant-garde. Except for the activities of a few publications involved with conceptual art, like *Vile* or *Northwest Mounted Valise*, most experimentation in magazines seems internecine or elaborately involved with the play of precedents discussed earlier. Concretism came into American magazines late and was introduced here by a university magazine (*Chicago Review*). As far as I know, there was never a magazine in this country comparable to Ian Hamilton Finlay's *Poor. Old. Tired. Horse.* or a publishing program like Agenzia in France. The most intense literary experimentation in the last decade has been in fiction, and the economics of magazine publication kept most of the little magazines out of the center of these activities. There was also an area of conflict between the new fiction and small pressmanship. In addition to demanding increased expenditures for typesetting and paper, the new fiction's antirealism became the focus for charges of social elitism that poetry—its mantle of sentimental individualism and licensed narcissism still intact—was spared. Fiction, it seems, invokes a politics from which (sadly) poetry has been excused. When I was a director of CCLM, I was accused in public of being antirealist, and therefore elitist, by a small-magazine editor who in the previous breath had proclaimed himself a member of the avant-garde and one of the few true heirs of the modern magazine tradition. If the new fiction wanted magazines, it would have to make its own.

In the 1960s little-magazine publishing, like much of the rest of the culture, was suffused in politics. Poets who would never have spoken to one another on literary grounds were allied in readings against the war in Vietnam, and there was a companion solidarity among magazines. As in the general culture also, there remains in the magazine world a residual leftism, focused occasionally on conservation or on a particular struggle, which surfaces in literary discussion here and there. Institutions are still distrusted. A populism never required of poetry is frequently demanded of fiction, and experimental fiction is seen as dangerously self-involved. The editor's inherent interest in production and distribution veers dangerously close to capitalism. With all the cosmological froufrou of the Whole Earth Movement, do-it-yourself printing and binding is often raised from its place as economic necessity to a level of singular and unassailable virtue. As I suggested before, the magazine boom requires sociology as much as it does criticism or literary history. There are basic contradictions between the obvious goals of most magazines and the political sentiments that seem native to meetings of little-magazine editors, and are part of the relationship of literature to the society as a whole. Magazine editors, as much as any group, are concerned about the dangers of growth. There is a sense among them that whatever it is that makes literature most valuable and vital cannot survive corporate climates and the manipulations of large amounts of money and resources. The problems are quite real, but the emotional recoil from them frequently results in limits set so close at hand that they make any development impossible. I have attended meetings at which any editor who talked about professionalized production or energetic distribution was hooted down as a sellout.

> *Where there are angels, there are*
> *wrangles, where there are editors,*
> *there are creditors . . . it is as*
> *simple as that.*
> —Cyril Connolly(1964)

**3**

Literary magazines are all failing business propositions. That any survive at all is a tribute to editors skilled at everything from typesetting to down-home flimflam. Traditionally, magazines were supposed to be supported by angels, creatures as implausible in contemporary literature as they are in modern theology. There are some magazines that still have benefactors left over from the fall of the patronage class. Some rely on university support—a financial base that has grown less dependable as universities themselves have lost much of their financial stability. It was once assumed that a university-based editor was on easy street; now he has to be seen as someone deftly juggling a small morsel above a tank of piranha. The majority of contemporary magazines are supported almost entirely by the editors—in cash and labor. Even with the infusion of editorial labor, most magazines have fairly high unit costs; magazines with cover prices of a dollar to a dollar and a half frequently cost two or three dollars to produce and distribute. Some larger magazines can manage better cost figures because of larger print runs, but distribution barriers seem to exist that keep them from taking advantage of favorable numbers. Simply put, all magazines need money, and money for literature is hard to get. Foundation support for literature nationally is less than 1 percent of all grants made, and the National Endowment manages less than 2 percent.

Literature is altogether too private, both in its production and consumption, to gather the support given to operas, orchestras, theater companies, and ballets. There are no opera house overheads, no unions, no guarantees, no advance ticket sales, and, finally, no grand openings to ooze social prominence and drip jewelry.

Since 1967 the Coordinating Council of Literary Magazines has served as a grant-giving agency for literary magazines, distributing funds from the Endowment and a few private sources. Because the organization deals in funding magazines and has a large membership, it is a good context in which to test the possibility of cooperation suggested by my friend the Russian editor. If the total consolidation of production, distribution, and editorial judgment he had in mind are both impractical and undesirable in our situation, some sense of common purpose once seemed possible through CCLM. The grants program brought the magazines together, however churlishly. The initial notion was to fund quality magazines according to their needs. The idea never sat well with the small-magazine editors, who argued that because of large costs of big magazines, they would get all the money. Figures sailed back and forth between CCLM and COSMEP, a coalition of small magazine and small-press editors, with attendant accusations. Grants committees were elected from among the editors and writers involved with the magazines, but since the amount of money available in grants was never large enough, no one was ever really satisfied. No big magazine could ever hope to get a grant that would make a useful dent in its deficit; the smaller magazines were never persuaded that deficits were anything more than the numerical record of the capitalistic vices of larger magazines.

The fracture between large and small, in many ways unjustifiable on hard evidence, was fairly permanent. Also, the Endowment seemed eager to be swayed by the quarreling that went on, largely because the CCLM grant represented a large portion of Literature

Panel funds that had gone out of the Panel's control. The arena for charges, accusations, and threats simply expanded. Eventually the Endowment established two grants programs for magazines independent of the CCLM program.

The future of CCLM in the midst of such fractured funding is uncertain. Certainly the sort of magazine unity I had once thought possible has been foreclosed. The grants procedure has always posed a threat to the independence of the magazines, though it was hopelessly exaggerated by all the quarreling. If judgments were made on the basis of quality, then marginally, at least, the organization was monitoring the editorial content of the magazines. It was presumed that the elected grants committees would disarm this concern. They did not. The degree of distrust was so high that everyone involved was suspect. The final stage in the grants committee system was reached in 1977, when an elected committee decided that it would not make qualitative judgments of any kind. The funds were simply divided equally among all the applicants, giving each a grant of about $900. In this gesture some of the grantees received more than a year's total budget; others were stuck with far less than a meaningful sum of money. The organization, which had spent years building assurances of noninterference into the rules governing committee procedures, was forced to sit by and watch its basic assumptions about magazine funding fall victim to a single committee. Unity had come to mean equity, and equity finally became equivalency.

Quite apart from issues of literary quality, but in keeping with the populist attitudes within the organization, CCLM has undergone another set of strains on its potential unity. Along with the society as a whole, the organization has been forced into an awareness of minority needs. A program was established to bring minority magazines into the grants procedure early by waiving the three-issue rule. Affirmative action resolutions were passed. The scenario is a familiar one, but CCLM, more than most institutions, is ill suited to the situation. Its history has been completely involved with independent, highly individualistic operations, the literary equivalent of Jefferson's American frontiersman, nervous when anyone else has settled within ten miles. For political and social reasons, minority magazines tended to be the work of coalitions. A very nearly atomized pluralism that had just been served by replacing judgment with long division was being asked to deal with a series of collectivist groups. Although the goals of ethnic literary magazines were acceptable, the nature of their demands was dangerously close in dollars to the amounts requested by larger magazines, but in this instance accusing the magazines of rampant capitalism seemed implausible.

Because CCLM had been involved primarily with editors and their magazines, their needs came to overshadow the concern with writers and their work. Magazines can easily become their editors' primary form of self-realization—peculiar monads of intense self-reflexivity. The tendency is probably endemic and not altogether bad, for it carries some of the essential brave lunacy that keeps editors and magazines going. Still, it is hardly conducive to organizational strength. When self-realization is a primary goal, then one self-realization is as good as any other; the more liberal sanctity a demand has, the less likely it is to be treated in any sort of measured way. The alternatives are simply capitulation or self-serving retreat.

Like the welfare system, CCLM has identified a community it has neither the resources nor the will to serve. It has made enough effective grants at lower levels to insure the marginal survival of much of its burgeoning population, but in the process has generated a new range of expectations that it cannot fulfill. All this could be an incentive to positive action if some sense of common purpose could be agreed upon. A Disneyland without Disney's resources, my

Russian friend might argue—a system of illusions at the point of
collapse, praising its own tatters as signs of virtue.

> *Nothing much then in the way of sights*
> *for sore eyes. But who can be sure who*
> *has not been there, has not lived there,*
> *they call that living, for them the spark*
> *is present, ready to burst into flame, all*
> *it needs is preaching on, to become a*
> *living torch, screams included.*
> —Samuel Beckett

**4**

The questions posed by my Russian friend—*Why are there so many
magazines? Who reads them? Why aren't there fewer magazines with more
readers?*—are troublesome because they sit so readily among the
anxieties I have had about them as a writer, editor, and . . . what's
a good term for a CCLM director? . . . strategist (perhaps). They
also play evil tricks with the deformations of my own nostalgias. I
have a fondness for the magazines of the first half of the century. I
keep them around—not a collection, nothing so orderly as that, just
a scattering of things: a few *Poetrys* from 1913, a *Horizon* from 1944,
some early *Partisan Reviews*, some few *Botteghe Oscures*, a *Dial* from
1929. What I do have in sequence begins in the 1950s when I started
subscribing. The earlier things are talismans, magical remnants of a
world made orderly, even heroic, in retrospect. The great magazines of that era seem so singular that, taken one by one, they
suggest an overall clarity of literary purpose that could never have
existed.

Of course, the Russian did not understand the import of that
stack of magazines he could not keep upright. How could he? Their
significance so easily eludes *us*. The answers to his questions are
altogether too simple to give us much comfort. *Why are there so*

*many?* Because that's how it is for a literature committed to change. Literary magazines today fill the same functions they filled at the beginning of the century. They give a place to writing for which no other place has been made. Criticism is slow and cautious; popular taste, as important as it is in other contexts, has nothing to do with the development of writing; commerce is too cautiously trying to pace a slow criticism to quixotic popularities. The world of literary magazines is raffish and irregular because nothing else will do in a setting in which the best hope of every serious writer is to undermine every notion of what makes a piece of writing good and durable.

Of course there are too many magazines. The genius that magazines have shown for graceful dying has not been entirely lost, and it should be cultivated. Yet the magazine explosion, finally, is not the fault of editors or national endowments but of writers. More and more we have drawn the magazines to our various isolations, instead of moving on, as we should, into riskier associations. If the magazine community is past fragmentation and nearer atomization, so are its writers. The magazines have always moved with writers. In our fear of any authority we have accepted a certain protective diffusion, and the magazines have responded by replicating and amplifying that diffusion in ways which make authority nearly impossible. In a symbiosis refined to neural complementarity, they serve our fears as well as our more cogent desires.

*Who reads magazines, anyway?* Again the answer is too simple. Editors and writers, mostly, and a few stray fans. Some of the larger magazines have enormous impact. Most small magazines are communications among contributors. In a CCLM survey of magazine subscribers, we found the readers are largely writers, then teachers, followed by librarians and students. Most are highly educated and underpaid, not the sort of community that would make for a good advertising sales campaign. Perhaps magazines that have very small readerships are occasionally read by editors of magazines with larger readerships; it's hard to know. In some instances, magazines serve largely as the medium through which writers give their work its public gesture—that crucial, if phantom, reader out there who is often important chiefly as a hypothesis.

The Russian's last question is the one I have spent the most time puzzling over, here and elsewhere. I became involved with CCLM in the conviction that some unity among magazines could be fashioned which could be a service to them without getting in their way. Obviously, we cannot have a *Young Guard* taking the place of our fifteen hundred magazines. Throughout the century, American literature has taken its vitality from its own extreme edges, since its center is too often lifeless and boring. This last is not only a corollary of the tradition of the new; it has to do, as well, with the desperation with which status is held onto in a society that claims not to value status. Without the graduated steps of a writers' union and an official publishing bureaucracy, we cling to our little tracts of notoriety with all the tenacity and imagination of suburbanites. American letters can survive only by confronting change, and the magazines serve as both belfry and rampart in this essential confrontation.

## 13

## Harriet Monroe's Skyscraper

In 1891, Harriet Monroe presented herself to the formidable Committee on Ceremonies for the World's Columbian Exposition to argue that poetry should have some place in the fair. Music, art, and architecture had already been included. Why should poetry be left out? The combination of conviction, ingenuousness, tenacity, and social influence that charmed most of her life won the day. In October 1892, with an orchestral setting and a chorus of 5,000 voices, her "Columbian Ode" was read at the dedication of the fair. The Vice-President of the United States crowned her with a laurel wreath. She was 31 years old, an enthusiastic but largely unsuccessful conventional poet, and the daughter of a respected Chicago attorney. Twenty years later, with the same kind of conviction that she took to the Exposition committee, she founded *Poetry, A Magazine of Verse*, the most distinguished and durable literary magazine                                                                    of the 20th century.

From its first issue (October 1912), *Poetry* was unique. It was the first of the modern literary magazines. Most of what followed existed with reference to it. *Others, The Little Review, Broom, The Glebe*, and the other magazines of the teens all took their impetus from *Poetry's* success. The record of the magazine is unparalleled. Most of the major poets of the century have appeared in its pages, and an amazing number can be claimed as *Poetry* discoveries. The magazine's first years included work by Ezra Pound, Robert Frost, W. B. Yeats, Edwin Arlington Robinson, William Carlos Williams, H. D., T. S. Eliot, D. H. Lawrence, Wallace Stevens, Carl Sandburg, Vachel Lindsay, and James Joyce. Although her "Open Door" policy and a genuine affection for traditional work kept *Poetry* technically diverse, Harriet Monroe was a champion of the free-verse movement and at the center of the controversy over modernist versification. The magazine was quickly identified with the "new poetry" and was praised, parodied, attacked, or merely noted with curiosity in newspapers from Chicago to Shanghai.

Harriet Monroe edited *Poetry* until her death in 1936. In retrospect, her first years seem to be the most exciting, but her durability and continued openness to new work are also impressive. Throughout the 1920s, *Poetry* continued to publish new work by its original contributors, and it introduced Yvor Winters, Ernest Hemingway, Louise Bogan, Hart Crane, Archibald MacLeish, Robinson Jeffers, and Stanley Kunitz. In the 1930s, Basil Bunting, Langston Hughes, Allen Tate, W. H. Auden, Stephen Spender, Dylan Thomas, and Theodore Roethke came into the magazine. Monroe's assertion that poets needed a forum that was "free as air" had, by the time she died, created a literary institution that could survive without her.

In its 66 years, *Poetry* has had weak moments. It was never an unbroken string of masterpieces. From the first issue, it published its share of mortal poems, even its share of bad poems. Mistakes are inevitable in magazines; accepting their likelihood is all that keeps any editor from falling victim to the paralyzing scrutiny of as-yet-unborn critics and anthologists. Good magazines play to their own present with enough energy to push back at it when it becomes restrictive. *Poetry* has remained a great magazine because it has changed over the years—changed editors and points of view.

In the late thirties and forties, it was edited by a group of Chicago writers. The period lacks the flash of the early years, but it was a less dynamic period in poetry, as well. The editorial group included Peter DeVries, George Dillon, Marion Strobel, and Morton Dauwen Zabel in varying combinations, all able custodians. The magazine's next long-term individual editor was Karl Shapiro (1950–1955). Shapiro's term produced a run second in brilliance only to Monroe's first years. With the assistance of Isabella Gardner, he gave the magazine as much range and acuity as it has ever had. Like Monroe, Shapiro came at a time when poetic activity was energetic and diverse. He published the best work of established poets and was open, as well, to new, radically different writers. Shapiro also published a great deal of foreign poetry in translation.

Under Henry Rago (1955–1969), *Poetry* flourished, but it lacked the focus it had had with Shapiro. In addition to his own interests, which were fairly broad, Rago felt, perhaps too keenly, a responsibility to be representative; leafing through his issues, you can feel the strain of an eagerness to meet the demands of an expanding poetry scene. Daryl Hine's tenure (1969–1977) seems, by comparison, a retrenchment. Hine's technical standards were high, and his tolerance for the extreme personalism and sentimentality of much of the late-sixties poetry explosion was low. Both dispositions tended to take *Poetry* out of the center of things, and they lost the magazine much of the allegiance that it had always commanded from poets. Still, Hine's editorship had its own lusters; he published, sometimes rather boldly, complex longer poems by both established and less well-known writers, and in a period crowded with hundreds of competing magazines, he published more than a fair share of major work by John Ashbery, Kenneth Koch, James Schuyler, James Merrill, Charles Wright, and John Matthias, among others.

Hine left the magazine at the end of 1977, after completing his editorial work on *The Poetry Anthology 1912–1977* with the help of

Joseph Parisi, the magazine's associate editor. The anthology aims at giving readers a retrospective view of *Poetry's* first 65 years, a monumental job of reading and selecting. In his introduction, Hine takes on the double burden of being both representative—reclaiming for the magazine's masterpieces something of their original settings—and of selecting all the poems on their own merits. The first task is historical, the second critical, and the two aren't always compatible. Criticism, no doubt, excluded Joyce Kilmer's "Trees," but for historical reasons it could well have been included. It would have dramatically characterized the magazine's early variety. In large part, though, the earlier period is well represented, its dazzle still intact; the major pieces are all here—"Prufrock," the first of Pound's *Cantos*, Robinson's "Eros Tyrannos," Steven's "Sunday Morning," Williams's "Le Médecin Malgré Lui," Sandburg's "Chicago," and Yeat's "Prayer for My Daughter." Choices in the later periods are less obvious, but a sense of the magazine is maintained throughout. Among the happy surprises (all anthologies, however ponderous, need surprises) are the number of first-rate poems by writers we know mostly in other contexts—early poems by Ernest Hemingway, John Dos Passos, Harold Rosenberg, and Leslie Fiedler among them.

The representation of the period of Henry Rago's editorship and Daryl Hine's invites the most quibbling, if only because the work is so contemporary. The absence here of James Wright and Charles Olson, from opposite ends of the poetry of the fifties and sixties, is a flaw, as is the exclusion of Galway Kinnell from the section on the sixties, a period when he published significant work in *Poetry*. Most curious, though, is Hine's anthology version of his own term as editor. Some of his really brilliant strokes are missing; perhaps the publisher restricted his use of longer work. In place of major John Ashbery poems, such as "Fragment" and "Self-Portrait in a Convex Mirror," we get "A Man of Words"; the longer Koch poems he published are also missing, as is Charles Wright's "Skins" and James McMichael's "The Vegetables." The work of John Matthias, who found in *Poetry* his one solid American home, is absent altogether. The closing selection is more puzzling than it is weak. For whatever reason, in his valedictory, Hine seems to have forgone his strongest editorial suit.

The anthology is no substitute for leafing through the magazine itself, but it does give a sense of the history of modern poetry and its premier publication that is hard to come by in any other way. It should be met with some pride in Chicago. The magazine is a Chicago institution, as much as as the Art Institute and the Symphony. Harriet Monroe founded the magazine with the support of a hundred prominent Chicagoans, who agreed to subscribe for five years at $50 a year. She had hoped that by then the magazine would be self-sufficient. Instead, both she and the magazine she founded had become justly famous, and her board of guarantors continued to support her. This relationship, between a magazine and a city, is unique, as far as I know, to *Poetry* and Chicago. In a very real sense, this connection made the magazine possible and has sustained it. Most literary magazines last a year or two and then die. The five years that Harriet Monroe got from her patrons established the publication, and the existence of the guarantors made it possible for the magazine to continue after its founder's death. In a recent interview, Karl Shapiro said that *Poetry* could only have come into being and lasted so long in Chicago, in part because at the beginning of the century there was a genuine Midwestern poetry movement that Harriet Monroe could use as ballast to what came to her from London and New York, but also because no other city would have taken up a magazine, as it did museums and orchestras, as an extended social and cultural obligation.

*Poetry* still appears monthly, edited by the Chicago poet John Frederick Nims, who served on the editorial board in the forties and as guest editor in 1960. It is unlikely that *Poetry*—or any other magazine, for that matter—will ever again hold the center of literary attention that it held from 1912 to 1920; there are too many magazines in the field and too many writers published in such diverse ways. We can still hope, though, for a *Poetry* that is both open and authoritative, both exacting and "as free as air." The danger for any editor of *Poetry* is in sanctifying the history presented by this anthology too completely, in making the magazine and its imprimatur too hallowed for either freedom or daring.

One of the magazine's early critics said, "Miss Monroe led us to suppose she was building a cathedral—now it appears that it was a Woolworth Building." In her reply she said, "A cathedral, did I? Modern cathedrals are second-rate—mere imitations. I would rather build a first-rate skyscraper!" It is an appropriate figure for the magazine. Chicago has made two grand contributions to 20th-century art—the Chicago School of architecture, skyscrapers included, and *Poetry* magazine.

# 14

## Poetry:

## The Remarkable Thing is That There is So Much of It

One of the most remarkable things about contemporary poetry is how much there is of it. For an age most often characterized as mundane and commercial that seems unlikely, particularly since the poet is still romantically defined by the general society as an emotionally risky outsider. Still, poetry is being written everywhere by people as varied as the population itself. In colleges poetry writing classes are now more popular than poetry reading classes. In fact, it generally seems true that more people are writing poetry than reading it.

The 1975 edition of the *Directory of American Poets*, which includes only living poets whose work has been published in the U. S. and which has an application procedure and a committee to review the quality of the work of new applicants, has 1500 poet entries. Fifteen hundred officially designated, published, carefully selected poets moved, however slightly, toward the middle of the society by the very process of having their names, addresses, and phone numbers listed in this book. Out beyond that 1500 there are hundreds of thousands of poets who write occasionally, submit incessantly, and remain dejectedly unofficial. Contemporary poetry is Aristotle's dragon, so large and so different in its parts that there is no way to see the whole of it at once and no way to comment with any assurance on the full creature from the portion you happen to be able to see.

Early this summer, I had the fancy that if I sat down with the poetry books that were sent to the *Tribune* for review this year, I could comment on the general state of things and on the interesting books that surfaced among them. So, through several ozone alerts, I have positioned myself in the middle of several large stacks of slender books, shuffling, reading, restacking, and shuffling some more. I had visions of a kind of poetic archaeology for the geological horizon 1975 and the steady apprehension that what would come of it all would sound more like the transcript of a guided bus tour of an unfamiliar and not terribly notable city.

My impulse to keep everything together, good and bad, did not last very long. Shuffling very quickly becomes sorting, but even that gave me a much longer view than I usually take of several poetic subgenres.

The largest group is all more or less related to the Rod McKuen phenomenon, and the books are produced, always expensively, by reputable publishers who know a good-sized market when they see one. Most of these are feigned poems that take advantage of every conceivable poetic license toward sentiment and cliche. They are about loneliness and love and the consolations of true feelings sensitively presented. Reading through several is like being trapped in the linguistic aftermath of a thousand encounter groups: "I believe in you/You need me./You believe in me./I need you"; "I want to get back to the Harmonious Us"; "I mean I really do have some fears"; "You and that special May day"; and, quite literarily, "I remember January with someone who liked Baudelaire."

My students occasionally turn up with these books in response to class assignments; it's not very easy to say quickly and precisely why they are so bad to someone whose entire interests in poetry the breathless manners of such poets exhausts. They are like bubble gum rock, I say, trying to embarrass them into looking a little further for the "hard stuff." Some have photographs, and a rather specialized class of love poems, always written by handsomely tousled young men, feature photos of young women in various nonsexual exuberances on facing pages.

The quality of those photographs and the bland sexual suggestiveness of the poems say more about the state of yearning in America than half a dozen sexual advice columns and a clutch of X-rated movies.

Another subclass of poetry books is generated by the poetry therapy movement. These are poems to be used in therapy or poems written in therapy sessions. According to poetry therapist Jack Leedy, M.D., and the 13 psychiatrists and psychologists who contributed essays to Leedy's *Poetry the Healer*, poetry therapy is a successful, even essential, part of therapy in institutional settings. So add poetry in therapy to poetry in the schools, poetry to the people, and poetry in old people's homes. As helpful as I am certain it is, poetry therapy gives me the creeps. Imagine—"Nurse, put this patient on 40 mg Valium and two Elizabethan sonnets." That's not how it works, but that image or ones from John Barth's *The End of the Road* are inescapable.

Sooner or later the saving elitisms, however carefully broadened, return. Despite the amusements of giving the terrain in this way, it's serious poetry I like, or is it? Sort out all the McKuenists, the therapists, and the shortline photojournalists of pleasant rural scenes and what remains is serious and official, certainly, but serious and official can also be leaden and overprivileged. It is embarrassing and not a little frightening to notice how often good, accomplished poets can be bad and how easily the modern virtues—terseness, physical images carefully rendered, plain diction, and surreal surprise— grow conventional and dull, as cant as the 19th-century excesses they replaced. Still, there is a lot that is remarkable and exciting and different enough to make our fondness for openness and variety seem more than just an excuse for a shambles. There are books that find their way to the top of these stacks, however they are sorted and shuffled.

John Ashbery's *Self-Portrait in a Convex Mirror* is one of the most impressive volumes published in recent years. Many of Ashbery's poems are about paintings, like the title poem, which offers its own meditative equivalent to Parmigianino's painted tour de force. Even the poems that are not specifically about art have a painted quality to them, incidental scenes caught with a completed momentary tableau; three figures in a boat on a river, for example, whose reflections in the water surround the boat they are in, hold that place as though set down in 19th-century watercolor. Finally, though, these poems are primarily concerned not with art but with time, perception, and affection. That's too curt, I'm afraid, to match these relentlessly thorough poems—thorough because they take up each of their concerns as though only their sustained attention could redeem the insubstantial, vague present in which they first arise. In their own way these poems have as much breadth of subject as anything being written and have an ease in language—sometimes conversational, sometimes elegant—that can sustain the most elaborate pictorial rendering as well as the casual fracturings of an afternoon in the country.

Daryl Hine's poems in *Resident Alien* share with Ashbery's the sense of crucial artifice. In Hine the distance between the poem as a made thing and any ostensible subject is more pronounced because of the extreme and open delight in the subtleties of craft, but there is more than an exercise of conventional skill at work here. Hine's temporary landscapes depend on plays of language that seem intent on testing persistently whether any of the poems can contain their own rifts of diction and curious turns of idiom. There is a mannerist skew to all of this, a disquieting torque within the carefully fashioned surfaces of poems; it plays thru the slant rhymes he uses and across his metrical line.

James Schuyler's *Hymn to Life* has more of the immediacy of situation and image to it that is associated with American poetry after William Carlos Williams. Schuyler shares with Williams a sense of the poetic sufficiency of ordinary things; like his friend Frank O'Hara, Schuyler has a way of allowing the quick, earnest chatter of personal relationships into his poems. Both strains are parts of a music that grows up easily out of what seems to be a simple, conversational address, one that just happens upon its descriptive precisions. The long title poem that closes the volume is particularly noteworthy for its prolonged lyric brilliance. Schuyler is a quietly spectacular poet, one of the best.

Of all the books at hand, the only one that approaches the directness and elegance of *Hymn to Life* is a translation from the Chinese, Burton Watson's rendering of the poems of Lu Yu, *The Old Man Who Does As He Pleases*. This enthusiasm is based not at all on an understanding of Chinese but on the skill of the poems as translated and on the informative generosity of Watson's introduction and his headnotes to the poems.

Two new books by poets associated originally with the Beat Movement in San Francisco still exhibit the explosiveness of language and the uninhibited use of rhetoric that gave the movement so much of its energy. William Everson's *Man-Fate: The Swan Song of Brother Antonius* is a sequence of love poems that involve Everson's leaving the Dominican order he had been part of for 20 years.

Michael McClure in *September Blackberries*, engages in a familiar clamor of type across the page, exploding capitals, and occasional diagonal lines. The immediate sense is of a play merely of volume, something aiming toward the primal scream that is mentioned on the dust-jacket. Fortunately there is more to it. McClure, at his best, manages a series of discoveries, and his language strikes with almost flint-like suddenness and brilliance.

For the last few years Anne Waldman has been engaged in experiments with the relationship of the poem to the poetry reading, composing for public occasions rather than merely writing poems that happen incidentally to be read in public. The title poem of *Fast Speaking Woman* is one of the most widely heard contemporary poems. These are chants that work a strange magic in repetition and variation, incantations made of ordinary speech that have a ritual energy and a solidly contemporary language. What is fresh and not a little startling about them is that they abandon entirely the sense of slow fashioning that most contemporary form wants to mark for us in exchange for the accumulated music of repeated line and phrase. The form has origins in the work of Kenneth Koch, borrowing its jazzy subtlety of variation, and in Ginsberg's more ecclesiastical chants.

The first sense of movement one has in Adrienne Rich's *Poems: Selected and New* is the press toward the political that has accompanied the development of her work, but this retrospective offers a great deal more. It is a general view of the work of one of our strongest poets. Rich has never been at ease with the materials of her poems or with her craft. What is exciting here, apart from the simple exhilaration of reading such poems as "Autumn Sequence," "Night in the Kitchen," and "Waking in the Dark," is Rich's willingness to have her most pressing personal and political concerns fracture accomplished strains in her verse. The sense is of continuous invention, and the poems of radical feminism that conclude the collection are part of the incessant change.

I was initially displeased with Diane Wakoski's new book, *Virtuoso Literature for Two and Four Hands* for what seemed to be a new fondness for enclosing metaphors and embellished narrative. I still dislike the title poem but have grown increasingly fond of the rest of the collection, especially the shorter poems, which have an economy and surprise about them. There is more risk to Wakoski's use of the personal and confessional than in most poets. Her self-revelations are not simply subjects for poems which is quite often true in the work of others. Instead, each seems to threaten the existence of the sensibility at work on the poem. More carefully and economically set down than in her last book, the language of this collection is more durably redemptive of those occasions than anything we have had from her before.

There is more that I like left in the scattered piles of books, but I can only note them in passing. Charles Wright's *Bloodlines*, whose two long sequences, "Tattoos" and "Skins," are simply brilliant in their development of a form for surfacing images of the past in the personal present; Daniel Hofman's *The Center of Attention*; Linda Pasten's *Aspects of Love*; Albert Goldbarth's *Jan. 31*; and Michael Ryan's *Threats Instead of Trees*.

In addition to the individual collections of poetry done each year there are always a goodly number of anthologies. Only a few are historical or generic; most are gathered by subject. Among this last year's anthologies are collections of moon poems, open space (of the backpacking variety) poems, daughter poems, loneliness poems, love poems, patriotic and heroic poems, and therapeutic poems.

Two of the anthologies seem to me to have more than occasional significance. Taken together they also offer a sense of the range of what we call poetry. The first is *The Oxford Book of English Pastoral Verse* edited by John Barrell and John Bull. It is one of those thick, well-designed, and immaculately edited Oxford historical collections. The other is Bruce Jackson's *Get Your Ass in the Water and Swim Like Me: Narrative Poetry from Black Oral Tradition*. The temptation in most circles would be to treat Jackson's use of the word *poetry* with condescension and file the title under Folklore. Gathered mostly on tapes, from performers in Texas and Indiana prisons, these poems—or toasts, as they are called—are parts of a living oral tradition. They deal with the exploits of a number of stock characters—the trickster, the badman, and the pimp, among others. Many of the stories date from the 1930s; some are even older or represent specific variations on older tales.

Poetry exists always, it seems, between the extremes defined by these two anthologies. It is easy to be impatient with modern and contemporary poetry; for its complexity, its mad variety and its more than occasional disregard for its audience. In part it is difficult because it refuses to give up anything—the traditional, the oral, the pop, the sentimental, the learned, even the scientific. Offer a good modern poet the choice of the pastoral or the street corner conventions, and the poet will take both. It's that delusion toward completeness and sufficiency that makes American poetry such an adventure.

# 15

## The Poetry Wreck

Depending on your taste in poetry, you can either honor or blame Karl Shapiro for inventing one of the most common forms of the postwar American poem. He managed it in his first book, *Person, Place and Thing* (1942), a poem of mundane contemporary experience that jostled traditional poetic manners with contemporary subject matter and popular language. That sounds entirely too technical; the achievement had more to it than technical skill. That balancing of languages balanced, as well, indignation (or at least poetic distance) on one side with a pure American fascination on the other.

For a poet in America in the forties and early fifties and for much of poetry's readership it was a crucial invention, because it provided a form for the liberal imagination in poetry. Enough of the poetic quality of pre-20th-century verse was retained to secure the poet's place of refined observation and judgment; enough involvement, even delight, was reserved for the contemporary to make the poem acceptably a part of the mixed fascination and dread we have for the junk that lies all about us. Seen in purely formal terms, this was a retreat from modernist experimentation. Socially and culturally, it was a cautious but deliberate move to the left, away from the cultural aristocracy of so much of early modernism.

I linger over Shapiro's early poetry, however briefly, because it is the one way that the sense of grievance that broods over his essays can be given a useful context. *The Poetry Wreck* gathers Shapiro essays from three previous critical books along with some recent articles and addresses. Most of the material is well-known; some of it is even notorious. The arrangement of the essays, the brief foreword, and the title give the book a kind of thesis that we might not otherwise expect from a *selected* volume.

For Shapiro 20th century poetry began with a conspiracy and is ending in a shambles. The *wreck* of his title is mangled at both ends. The collection opens with three essays from *In Defense of Ignorance*, which attack the reputations of T.S. Eliot, Ezra Pound, and W.B. Yeats, "the Great Trio" (Shapiro is fond of capitalized labels) of modernist poetry. The book ends with a recent essay on popular poetry in the late sixties, which focuses on Dylan Mac-Goon, an invention that allows Shapiro to avoid mentioning Rod McKuen's name and also generalize him a bit, attacking, as well, the illiteracies of much contemporary writing and the eagerness on the part of so many professors and critics to accept anything at all as a poem.

The essays on Pound and Eliot were extremely controversial when they first appeared in print, in the late fifties. People aligned themselves with Shapiro or with the *masters*. There was, even if you disagreed with him, a kind of electricity in Shapiro's willingness to take on such giants. It is disappointing to read them again. The pieces on Eliot and Pound are so laden with conspiracy and its attendant paranoias that they are simply hard to get through. Literary conspiracies make good cocktail party conversations because they tend to capture everyone's attention; they do very little for criticism. On reflection, we should all admit to being would-be conspirators insofar as we all set out to make our own tastes and our own work infectious.

What survives these pieces' contentiousness is Shapiro's concern over the antiquarianism and cultural prescriptiveness of these
moderns. All three offered architectonic alternatives to the degra-
dations of the present that were based in remote and repressive
orthodoxies. For Shapiro and many of his contemporaries they
were surely fearsome edifices. It is important to remember that
Shapiro is a member of the first generation of American poets
schooled entirely under the dominance of modernism as it was
defined by these three poets in general and by T.S. Eliot in
particular. In a very real sense, though, the essays are gratuitous.
Shapiro's earliest poems made a far more effective gesture, which
was later consolidated in his own stylistic development. I am not
saying that Shapiro improved on these poets or that he was
revolutionary but that he made a significant adjustment that could
account for his experience as something other than a bad example.
It is a measure of the insecurity of 20th-century poetics that an
attachment to the cultural values of the past was replaced only by
rather firmly lodging the poem's form and at least a part of its
diction in the 19th century.

*The Poetry Wreck* includes several enthusiastic essays. Those show
Shapiro at his critical best, not because enthusiasm alone makes
good criticism but because it relieves him of the invective that
burdens the opening group. The piece on William Carlos Williams
is probably Shapiro's best treatment of another poet. His discussions
of Dylan Thomas, D.H. Lawrence, and Henry Miller are as positive, but with Williams Shapiro settles into the concern he shares
with Williams over the making of a form for poetry that can deal
directly with American experience; as a result he is extremely
helpful in dealing with Williams' unevenly presented theories of the
poetic line. All of these positive pieces have a commitment to the
aesthetic rebel that occasionally moved toward celebration.

The sense is that Shapiro, in his essays anyway, sees himself in the same role. In a loose but attractive address called "American Poet?", in which Shapiro was asked to talk about himself, he says that he thinks of himself not as a critic but as someone who responds to an invitation "with gusto and sassiness." Fair enough.

But this selection has another ambition, the exhibition of the *wreck* referred to in the title and sketched out in the foreword. Classic modernism has been under attack from several sides. The earliest and most sustained dissent came from Yvor Winters, whose *In Defense of Reason* Shapiro inverted for his *In Defense of Ignorance*. A more recent assault by Leslie Fiedler in an essay called "The Children's Hour" is at once closer to Shapiro's and instructively different in its conclusions. Fiedler sees modernism as elitist and pretentious, not merely reactionary but actually divisive; what he wants in its place is an unobstructed love for the sentimental and the popular—the sentimentalities of Longfellow and rock lyrics, free of the self-imposed bondage of modernist intellectualism, what he calls "the Terror." Fiedler, as ever, follows the argument to its end. Shapiro wants off at a much earlier station. He is as offended by the rabble poetry of the late 1960s as he is by the elitisms of the 1920s and has a special disdain for academics, such as Fiedler, who quote rock lyrics as poetry and participate in what Shapiro calls "cultural barbarism."

Shapiro's double disdain, past and present at each end of the scale, is curious only schematically. What is ironic is that so much of Shapiro's prose through the years seemed to champion the poetic explosion he now abhors. The focus on Rod McKuen in the title essay is misplaced. McKuen serves his audience, as large as it is, by his own low-grade pretentiousness. He has supplanted Gibran in much the same way that those fuzzily focused $1.00 photographic greeting cards have replaced the old ones that had stuffed satin faces. His influence is far less great than that of the Beats, who were once potential models for Shapiro's venturesome sense of ignorance, except that the surviving Beats now share with their audience an eagerness for the arcane, now grounded in the Oriental, the occult, or the anthropological detailings of the primitive.

There is, indeed, a new illiteracy, but its most frightening feature is to be found not among the standard college English teacher gripes Shapiro repeats here but in the simple fact that there are now more people writing poetry than reading it. Imbedded somewhere in that fact is the sense that being a poet, the idea (notion, perhaps) of being a poet is most important and that the poem, fully disassociated now from the role being played, has fallen down into the heap of discarded values.

As literary situations go, this is commercially unattractive, certainly. It threatens to replace the book with the workshop—employment security versus a readership. But it is also attractive in a variety of ways. There are too many poets or quasi-poets, but there are also many good and exciting poets working without the oppression of the kind of literary orthodoxy against which Shapiro once fought. More attractive still is the devaluation of the poem as icon, that unassailable, organic thing that has been hauled out like a sacred relic in classrooms and critical essays and offered incantations of the Socratic Catechism or the exegetics of the critical method. Let it suffer a little from casual attention or overpopulation; it will survive. What is required of those of us who practice the art is what has always been required, plus not a little patience and more tolerance than we are perhaps used to.

## 16

## "O Lana Turner we love you get up"

American poetry has made a number of approaches to what it presumed was ordinary speech—Whitman's *democratic speech*, Williams's *American idiom*, and recently the *language of the streets*. Like politicians clamoring against each other in the same rhetoric of freedom, justice, and progress, poets arguing for iambic meter, triadic measure, and free verse frequently claim the patterns of ordinary speech as their own. Plain talk, infrequently the aspiration of poets, is the ground on which most American poets claim to play. There are historical precedents for this, obviously, but modernism peculiarly both heightened and thwarted the desire for the vernacular. The assaults on meter and poetic diction can be seen as assertions of the ordinary. The "musical phrase" of Pound's Imagism presumed intrinsic poetic qualities in language, despite the fact that in Pound the music was more often orchestrated out of the archaic. The more exaggerated assumptions of Williams and the Objectivists begin with the same principle, however. The concurrent interest in the stuff of perception, the 'thingy-ness' of language and the distrust across several poetic schools of abstractions created a set of compositional practices in poetry that made its ordinary language a very limited version of speech. Exaggeration, exclamation, poetic diction (in the 19th century sense), and high sentence were all set aside for the best of reasons. It still makes good sense to "go in fear of abstractions," but common speech has no poetic traditions it needs to kill off. The diction of anti-poetic poetics became, in its own turn, as specialized and distinctly *poetic* as the O's and Ah's of the past. Today, the average poem in an American magazine is as predictable as the work in a William Stanley Braithwaite magazine verse anthology in the teens.

Rigorously applied, the taboos of modernist composition limited access to a great deal of speech. Concrete detail may save the poet from the conventionally vague, but its danger is myopia. Plain diction protects the poet from the artificially emotive but has as well an insulation against the lovely slouch and exaggeration of mere talk. Free verse has its own doggerel, a deadly acceptance of the breaks and pauses of the sentence that are always manipulated to good effect by any emphatic speaker. The ordinary in poetry risked being—often became—merely plain and not the least bit like talk.

What the austerities of poetry avoided Popular Culture managed with a vengence. Without any prescriptions but the need to catch attention and be instantly memorable popular songs and, later, commercials and movies were both excessive in coventionally poetic ways and enormously reflexive to the adjustments of the language. It is surprising—perhaps less so to an audience like this one than to a poet—how much the aspirations of the commercial and the poem have in common. The commercial offers a language into ordinary occasions—bad breath, yellow teeth, a dull kitchen floor—whose rhapsodic moments are to be retained to the point of sale; it has somehow to encompass a language like our own as well as its jingle or its slogan—inescapable formulae for everyday anxieties. A part of the delicious unreality of the movies is their sprinkle of memorable speech that is archly contrived to resound past the limitations of a character. Like Busby Berkley routines involving hundreds of swimming dancers, pools, and waterfalls which the plot situates on the narrow space of a vaudeville stage, these speeches play against the characters who mouth them toward the movies' more extreme ambitions among our dreams of certitude, significance, clear moral dimensions, and intensity. They are made out of old rhetoric and familiar exaggeration, often bouncing down in the middle of a haphazard scene on the movie's own bizaare title. It is this delight in the extreme which has characterized the popular throughout the century. "Play it again, Sam" is a refrain of such incredible sentimentality that until recently no well-schooled poet would go near it, unless it could be bundled over with an acceptable irony or stand first as an allusion.

There have been a number of plays across the line between poetry and the popular in contemporary work. Recently, the border zone has become a place of important poetic transaction. Mac Hammond's superb sequence "The Horse Opera" offers in one of its late arias the best view I know of both territories and their equivalent tugs on the poet.

> I wish I was The Cowboy.
> I wish I were Cocteau.
> I wish I were Proust.
> I wish all my chickens
> would come home to roost.
> I wish I had a gun.
> I wish I were my son.
>
> I wish I may
> I wish I might
> Be the movie star
> I see tonight.

The two sides of this struggle even have their play in the grammar of the poem, a conflict of desire which is consumed—if not resolved—by the jingly rhymes that end it. Hammond's cowboy, who carries the poet's separate halves in his two holsters, quotes both Gary Cooper and William Butler Yeats. Like that phantom of light and shadow on the screen he is both cowboy and movie star—illusively real and persuasively fake. In his quest for either the poet is overburdened, "over-learned."

> Can't ride this horse, can't shoot this gun
> (It's the best horse, it's the best gun);
> I only look the part. A dude, a dud
> (I bought my duds at Brooks;
> My saddlebags are full of books)
> And parenthetical, pathetic, when The Badman
> Draws (highhand) and the Cowboy fires,
> I cringe, I crowd to the outhouse floor
> (The townsfolk laugh—"What is knowledge for?")
> I am overlearned, I know, I know

(Hammond's own saddlebags include a Harvard Ph.D. under Roman Jakobson and a study of the prosody of Wallace Stevens's "The Man With the Blue Guitar.")

Frank O'Hara's poetry plays across the boundaries of the popular with great ease, without the weight Hammond carries here. In O'Hara, a movie, a billboard, a candy wrapper, the sign caught in passing in the window of a diner come into the poem not as parts of a description but as particles of the poem's speech, full of all that extravagance poetry had eschewed, blaring in *National Enquirer* 72 pt. headlines, LANA TURNER HAS COLLAPSED. The language of headlines and especially the language of the movies carried back into the poem all of the castaway archness. Popular culture was the place where sentiment and exclamation held sway and were patinated with an unquestioned reality, a kind of validity as object. O'Hara's use of these materials is not really *camp*; it does not assume *camp's* trick of a patronizing distance. (I love this because it's so awful.) The

material is just there. It comes into and moves out of the work,
sometimes quite abruptly, often merely brushing against the poem's
other speech, as frequently, though, catching the poem with a fresh
velocity and turning it entirely.

POEM

Lana Turner has collapsed!
I was trotting along and suddenly
it started raining and snowing
and you said it was hailing
but hailing hits you on the head
hard so it was really snowing and
raining and I was in such a hurry
to meet you but the traffic
was acting exactly like the sky
a suddenly I see a headline
LANA TURNER HAS COLLAPSED
there is no snow in Hollywood
there is no rain in California
I have been to lots of parties
and acted perfectly disgraceful
but I never actually collapsed
oh Lana Turner we love you get up

There are a number of ways of coming back at this poem. What is
clear for our consideration today is that the headline has its own
presence here and that it takes command of the poem's other, more
personal urgency. The incipient love poem can be reconstructed by
analogy, unnamed "you" to Lana Turner, the presumption of hail to
the collapse, but what follows the headline in the poem is not so
easily exemplary. Within the rush of affection, weather, and city
traffic Lana Turner's collapse has a notable fixity, and all of the other
concerns in the poem are turned to it. The last line carries the weight
of the whole poem, of both urgencies, because its arch movie
voicing is capable of sentiment enough for both. The play of voice

is always important in O'Hara; this relatively early poem combines two kinds of speed—the rushed language of the street scene and the closing's exhortation. The revolutionary discovery of O'Hara's work rests within this sense of the voice of the poem, caught among the poem's occasions and, therefore, having to accept the pacing of occurance and sort through the city's "perpetuum mobile," to use Williams' term, for whatever significance happens to be available. This is the real sense of his play on John Donne—not *Meditations Upon Emergent Occasions* but *Meditations in an Emergency*. For O'Hara this process often lights on instances of popular language and mass imagery. Even at his greatest pace—in *Paterson I-IV* or in *Desert Music*—Williams's eye is always in search of the numinous object, the bright fragments of a broken, green bottle among the cinders, that will accept his iconic attention, that "so much" can, however arbitrarily, "depend upon" (to switch examples to that familiar red wheelbarrow). A beginning sense of O'Hara's major contribution to contemporary poetry can be gotten by thinking of the Lana Turner poem (titled, "Poem") as a complete deflection of the patterns of Imagism, which dominated poetry for so long.

When O'Hara addresses the movies directly, the poems are rhapsodic, taking up movie language entirely, even heightening the diction toward reverence. This is true of the several elegies to James Dean and delightfully of "To the Film Industry in Crisis."

> Not you, lean quarterlies and swarthy periodicals
> with your studious incursions toward the pomposity of ants,
> nor you, experimental theatre in which Emotive Fruition
> is wedding Poetic Insight perpetually, nor you,
> promenading Grand Opera, obvious as an ear (though you
> are close to my heart), but you, Motion Picture Industry,
> it's you I love!
>
> In times of crisis, we must all decide again and again whom we love.
> And give credit where it's due: not to my starched nurse, who taught me

how to be bad and not bad rather than good (and has lately availed
herself to this information), not to the Catholic Church
which is at best an oversolemn introduction to cosmic entertainment,
not to the American Legion, which hates everybody, but to you,
glorious Silver Screen, tragic Technicolor, amorous Cinemascope,
stretching Vistavision and startling Stereophonic Sound, with all
your heavenly dimensions and reverberations and iconoclasms! To
Richard Barthelmess as the "tol'able" boy barefoot and in pants,
Jeanette MacDonald of the flaming hair and lips and long, long neck,
Sue Carroll as she sits for eternity on the damaged fender of a car
and smiles, Ginger Rogers with her pageboy bob like a sausage
on her shuffling shoulders, peach-melba-voiced Fred Astaire of the feet . . .

and to all you others, the great, the near-great, the featured, the extras
who pass quickly and return in dreams saying your one or two lines,
my love!
Long may you illumine space with your marvellous appearances, delays
and enunciations, and may the money of the world glitteringly cover you
as you rest after a long day under the kleig lights with your faces
in packs for our edification, the way the clouds come often at night
but the heavens operate on the star system. It is a divine precedent
you perpetuate! Roll on, reels of celluloid, as the great earth rolls on!

With the movie stars in the poem, speaking or spoken too, the
conviction of specialized talk breaks down. "To the Film Industry in
Crisis" moves formulaically to its impossibly grand finale, a conceit
of metaphysical proportions. It is also possible for an O'Hara poem
to become a movie or be assimilated by various movies as it goes.
In later poems, like "Biotherm," movies quite casually enter the
mobile.

September 15 (supine, unshaven, hungover, passive, softspoken) I was very
    happy
                on Altair 4, I love you that way, it was on Altair 4 "a happy
                    day"
                I knew it would be
                yes to everything

135

I think you will find the pot in the corner
where the Krells left it
rub it a little and music comes out
the music of the fears
I reformed we reformed each other
being available
it is something our friends don't understand
if you loosen your tie
my heart will leap out
like a Tanagra sculpture
from the crater of the Corsican "lip"
and flying through the heavens
I am reminded of Kit Carson
and all those smiles which were exactly like yours
but we hadn't met yet
when are you going away on "our" trip
why are you melancholy
if I make you angry you are no
longer doubtful
if I make you happy you are no longer doubtful
what's wrong with doubt . . .

"Biotherm" is a long, freely textured poem. Here its speech is taken over by "Forbidden Planet," a "B" science fiction movie with Ann Francis, Guy Madison, and Walter Pidgeon, which has a moment's sway before attention returns to the lover's long monologue. Altair 4 works allusively, a distant idyllic planet once, long ago, inhabited by the superior race of Krells. Francis and Madison make good use of its pastoral and fall in love, while Walter Pidgeon, the anthropologist/mad scientist, dangerously puts on Krell knowledge, "the music of the fears." It's a strange Poundian vortex that is spindled on a "B" movie, stranger still that in the rush of the poem it seems not to matter; it is another of those briefly caught significances, more earnest than wise. Elsewhere, "Biotherm" gathers up overheard conversations, playbills, menus, and a host of characters from headlines, gossip columns, comics, and advertisements.

For O'Hara and a number of his contemporaries, especially in New York, movie stars, movie types, and even entire movies are the stuff of the common reference. They serve—as they do commonly enough anyway ("Well, she's an early Barbara Stanwyck type, if you know what I mean.")—as ready bundlings of conspicuous characteristics, like *the gods.* "After all," O'Hara wrote in "Personism: A Manifesto," only Whitman and Crane and Williams, of the American poets, are better than the movies."

What this radical view allows into poetry is not just Popular Culture as subject matter; it existed widely as subject in the work of the more established poets of the fifties and sixties. Familiar Karl Shapiro poems, like "Buick," "Haircut," and "Hollywood," are good examples. They digest these materials into a separate and, finally, distancing diction.

As a sloop with a sweep of immaculate wing on her delicate spine
Or even more typical of Shapiro's use of language—
    O wonderful nonsense lotions of Lucky Tiger
Or to press the contrast nearer to O'Hara's affections,
here's a piece of Shapiro's "Hollywood"—
    Farthest from any war, unique in Time,
    Like Athens or Baghdad, this city lies.

The concern, inevitably, of these skilfully mixed dictions is the security of the poet's place outside the materials being described. Such distances can be made with irony, nostalgia, or by a subtle overplaying of technique in the traditional sense. In O'Hara, Kenneth Koch, Edward Field, and to a lesser degree in poems by Gregory Corso and Allen Ginsburg and in recent work by a wide range of younger poets the popular enters the text with its material features still intact, clamoring into the field of attention instead of being held outside. To use the language of another, avante garde form, these elements are *found.*

In the work of younger contemporaries the access to the popular has been broadened and has grown more casual. Out of the easy domestic chatter of a recent Ted Berrigan poem we get—

> I'll never smile again!
> Bad teeth.

In Ron Padgett's work there is a sudden fondness for jingly, close rhymes. The repeated, structuring elements of Anne Waldman's new poems intrude into the text much like commercials cutting into a program. From Robert Sward we have the critical conviction that a single poem ought to operate like a cartoon and a sequence move like a comic book. There are, in fact, poets who now work exclusively in a comic book format, dangerously suggestive drawings included.

Here are three poets working in different ways with the vox pop. First, Anselm Hollo, the Finnish/British/American poet whose poems find a complete ease with the talk of commercials and street signs while adding, always, to an elaborate personal mythology. These are segments of a poem called "Art and Literature," Hollo's substitute for an assigned book review in the magazine of the same name.

> let me recommend
> the "Dennison" series of seals
>
> the 25¢ booklet
> "Cat Seals" in particular
>
> it contains a wonderful Persian:
> electric blue fur—& amber eyes—it's a classic!
>
> Gerry Gilbert has created a classic, too
> it's called 'phone book'
> you order it from weed/flower press
> 756 Bathurst Street Toronto Canada
> $1.50, & you should act *now*

★

staggering lives
the world loves
"The World Anthology"
but no one even likes "British Poetry Since 1945"
        which is just a roomful of music boxes
            confidently playing "Lara's Theme"
★

but one does like one poem in it,
Peter Pewter's haiku "Alone in The Kosmos"
it so brief one quotes:

    "i kneel by the infinite sands of the stars.
    my hat blows off the planet.
    dinner is in doubt."

Hollo's casualness is remarkable, and the equivalent play here of
the cat seals, plugs for the poet he likes, and the sharp parody of
the poets he doesn't aims at a fully opened idiom in the poem.
Hollo is not, however, merely talking. American idiom has a
perpetual surprise in his work that makes the poems intensely
comic but allows them, as well, fresh access to the mysteries
inherent in commercial language, mysteries which are polarized
into a pantheon Hollo has made for himself out of a variety of
religions.

The popular elements in Peter Michelson's work spill easily into
one another. Composing often from *found* materials, he keys the
poem into what is found, modulating the found material or
allowing it to begin a fun-house meditation on similar fragments.
"Whatever happened to Rita Hayworth" begins as a scenario for the
movie. "The Fire Down Below," but Rita Hayworth's presence
overcomes the scenario and the commentary the speaker wedges
into it.

        was that she said to Jack Lemmon      then
                                a punk kid

                    trapped
by a fallen steel girder
                        in the basement of      the U.S.S. Heart

                                of Darkness, where
                    he keeps stroking his beard and saying,
            "This too has been one of the dark places of the earth,"

                until Joseph P. Levine Presents,
            the producer, goes apeshit                shrieking
                "Punk,
shave that fucking beard,"        and kicks
        a steel girder which, this being
                                Hollywood, collapses on the kid . . .

            Miss Hayworth
        occasionally had delusions
of grandeur and thought she was Ava Gardner,    under which

                                        misinformation she
                    once married a Mexican matador, only to be
        deserted
when he moved up to Barcelona

            in the Three-I
        League, at which point she      thought she was

                        Marilyn Monroe and
        married an outfielder, who it turned out was good hit no
            field (or, as crazy
        Leonard used to chant—"Who
                can run and hit and throw / Better
                    than his brother Joe? / Why,
                        it's Dominic Dimaggio!), so . . .

Poems like this one presume a continuity of elements which the poem's rhetoric only needs to ride out. It is as though none of these characters, stars, baseball players, or film-clips had edges, they move so easily into one another. In a remarkable sequence of poems about the Indians of the Pacific northwest, "Pacific Plainsong," Michelson *finds* the manifest destiny rhetoric of the 19th century historian, H.H. Bancroft, working his distant, popular voice into a subtle version of the conquest of the Indians. Bancroft's righteousness keys the poems, and Michelson is often present only to play the self-justification back on itself.

I have been noting poets who *find* instances of the popular voice and variously let them take their tolls on their poems. In *Varmint Q* Charles Boer has made a narrative of astonishingly even texture without the jostle of harsh juxtaposition that operates in much of the poetry that used found language and the popular voice. *Varmint Q* is an epic poem on the life of William Clarke Quantrill that moves without any device you wouldn't expect from a dime novel account of Quantrill's life. Boer's informants chatter on as Frank Triplett's must have when the 19th century journalist was gathering material for the first biography of Jesse James. Boer wants pure story, unencumbered by cleverness and moving at the pace of excited talk. He includes letters, documents, and newspaper accounts from Quantrill's own day, and these sit easily with the rest of the poem's language. Charles Olson called the style of the poem "the annalic." Less cautiously, reviewers in Dodge City and Lawrence recommended the book to their readers, saying don't be bothered by the fact that this is poetry, you can read it anyway. Such backhanded compliments suggest that the poem has found out a successful popular idiom. It is interesting that it is the accomplishment of a poet widely known for his translation of *The Homeric Hymns* and *The Bacchae*—a fine classicist, a thorough student of both Pound and Olson, and a university professor of comparative literature, whose first book of poems, *The Odes*, was met with reverential, if puzzled, reviews.

There is the hint of a full circle here, which is more than a little tempting. It would be nice to say, quoting an obviously premature Williams poem, "The revolution is accomplished," to suggest that the search for the popular voice in poetry had reached its goal. The judgment would still be premature—and on several counts. Boer is not a typical contemporary poet; this is not likely to be a typical book, even from him. More importantly, the interface between the demotic and the poetic, however freely played, has not lost its attractiveness to poets. If it were to close, the poets would wedge it open, if not merely in search of a variety and tension in their address, then in response to changes in the two elements being faced off against one another. The movies, discussed so frequently here, have slipped from immediate view. One year's pop is the next year's trivia and the next year's nostalgia. The danger of popular elements, drawn into poetry for their free access to all, is that they can become so quickly allusive. *Varmint Q* is set in the past, a special past whose language we have already settled upon as a culture and whose mythology requires fine adjustments to our own changing habits but accumulates major revision very slowly. Finally, literacy, poetic literacy, in America still sits uneasily among a variety of aggressions. The poets with the largest audiences in this country are not among the group I have have discussed. Rod McKuen, Lois Wyse, and Dory Sherry do not write poems full of movies, billboards, or plain talk overheard; they write verse suited to—perhaps aimed at—a low-grade pretentiousness. McKuen's audience would be offended by O'Hara, Hollo, and Michelson; like the Kansas reviewers they might tolerate Boer by allowing the subject to obliterate their concern for the poetic-ness of poetry. Playing at the popular has always been radical business in American poetry. It bothers poets as much as poetry's sentimentally conservative readership. More than twenty years after the publication of his first book, Frank O'Hara is still (posthumously) one of the most radical and disruptive poets in this country.

Recently, one of my writing students said with some emphasis, "Our grandfathers were men of letters; we are not." He was paraphrasing Marge Piercy's call to relevance in *Literature in Revolution* (*Tri-Quarterly* #23). Just to be literal-minded, I took a census of the class. "How many of you have grandfathers you would call 'men of letters'?" No takers. "How many of you have grandfathers who are literate at all?" Four hands went up in a class of fourteen poets. Most of the time we shadow box a fictitious past populated by the creations of our own rhetoric. Our literary fathers and grandfathers grow real, and those painfully actual factory workers and gandy-dancers conveniently slide away, relegated to photograph albums and family reunions.

American poets have always carried too heavily the burdens of their own literacy, held it perhaps as arduously as they hold the continent, each day, on their shoulders. Pound's learning, however immense, always seemed uneasy; the form of the Cantos, in addition to being a positive, formal invention, is an accomodation to the lines of stress. Eliot's grand design is a piece-work of shards, so—for that matter—is O'Hara's mobile, though its elements are more readily at hand. We have a fine set of grandfatherly, even great-grandfatherly, men of letters, but their presence doesn't relieve the problem; it adds to it. They add to the trouble so many of us have being the first lettered people in our own immediate experience. They suggest—and often to good effect—an apprenticeship among dire complexity and oblique literary references. The desire for the popular among American poets remains doubled quite often with a desire for the arcane. What is interesting and exciting about the period we are in now is that the access on both sides is fairly free. Poetry escapes the tyranny of its precedents and its materials in the most casual use, by taking rather than borrowing.

The kinds of popular elements discussed here are not only a part of this broadened use; they have been crucial in making a new access possible. They have been used successfully to break modernism's limitations on the ordinary, and in Frank O'Hara's work, especially, have loosed the tie to the object.

## 17

## Another Dante

We live in an age desperate for cosmology, craving systems of belief, like yellow jackets fumbling for sugar in late summer. In the absence of anything everyone believes, we believe in anything— macrobiotics, Zen, est, tai chi, astral projection, astrology, andro- gyny, UFOs, vegetarianism, orgasm, Jim Jones, the right Reverend Moon, mushrooms, biorhythms, holistic healing, black holes, the whole earth, and a sort of wonder-drug Jesus who saves with the dazzling speed of injected steroids. None of these is ever supposed to be merely topical; each is required to serve a greater metaphoric purpose and strike some universal harmony. Books are written. Classes are held. And the legume's significance radiates through the moral and physical universe; the mushroom is the sacra- mental embodiment of spontaneous generation, nature's own Eu- charist; the UFO is evidence of our heritage among the gods; acupuncture and the *I Ching* prove that we are One. In the words of George Lucas's profitable, nonsectarian Sunday service, "May the Force be with you"—some force, any force, the force of your choice.

Reading Dante fresh (and freshness is, after all, the reward of new translations) in this climate is a complex pleasure. *The Divine Comedy* is the embodiment of a system of belief so complete that nothing in its world escapes it. All of human history, from antiquity to Dante' Florence, is here to be encountered in the ultimate form it has been given by divine judgment. In Dante's Hell torment endures, but it does not change. The characters of the *Inferno* are as they will be forever. There is no discordance between appearance and reality; appearance *is* reality, though the damned retain recognizable forms and continue to apologize and explain. The result is an idea of such thoroughness that its implications can be walked through and explored. What is discovered is not argued, but perceived.

By comparison, our metaphoric hankerings after unity seem nervous, even neurotic. If the body-in-harmony-with-nature is, as some would have it, the world's model and explanation, the connection has to be reasserted over and over again, in comparisons of widening scope. Even the Freudian universe, that most distinctly modern orthodoxy, requires persistent argument, the endless work of interpretation. Dante's journey has more to it than can be touched upon, more detail than he has time to scrutinize. Once Virgil, his guide and master, escorts him into Hell, Dante is a traveler, not a builder. His other-world is the manifestation of the philosophy, theology, and astronomy of his time, all bound by a coherence of belief and given shape by the poem, a poem of elaborate symmetries which moves in threes from syllable and stanza outward to a three-part whole of 100 (one plus 99) cantos.

All of this should make Dante extremely remote. He was a medieval man, after all, and the poem proceeds from a world so different from ours that it could easily be dismissed as an elaborately designed reliquary. But Dante, particularly in the *Inferno*, is surprisingly contemporary and accessible. In part, this is due to the effect the poem has had on the development of literature since it was written. Through a long succession of influences, including the very important role the poem has had in our own century, Dante continues to shape our sense of literature. Its accessibility is also due to the genius of the poem's most crucial invention, the traveler, speaker, explainer Dante. Dante the narrator gawks and recoils; he huddles toward Virgil for reassurance and protection, and we move with him as we read, leaning at Virgil's direction over every precipice, staring down into pockets of excrement for familiar faces. *The Divine Comedy* is an adventure of the human eye. Dante is forever looking, turning, scrutinizing. His attention to the physical details of the Inferno gives the poem its vibrancy and Hell its presence, but each of these excursions, adjustments, and readjustments of the eye confirms the presence of the perceiver. The effect is similar to what was produced in Italian painting a century later. Every painting in perspective is an assertion of the relevant presence of the eye of the painter, and every line of sight in Dante has the same result. It is this immediacy that impels us toward him, whatever our differences.

Dante's Hell has given shape to our general notions of what Hell is like. Even readers following Dante and Virgil through it for the first time will find it familiar. The Inferno is a great, terraced pit with nine descending circles to match the nine spheres of the medieval heavens. Its lower reaches are presented as a city whose architecture is in permanent ruin. For Dante, Hell was, among other things, a failed polity, more like the worst of modern cities than Milton's intricate Pandaemonium. Reverse the metaphor, and Dante's influence on modern urban literature becomes apparent. With few exceptions, the cities of modern literature are shaped to match this Hell, and excursions through them are successions of terrifying damnations.

The poet's first encounters are with virtuous pagans, the great poets of the past, but as he proceeds his experiences become more immediate. The Inferno is filled with Dante's Italian contemporaries. This would seem to make the poem idiosyncratic and remote, and school editions are filled with notes outlining Dante's personal and political relationships to the Italians he meets on the journey, but the final effect of Dante's insistence that Virgil find him "someone whose name or deed I recognize" is to bind the Inferno and the mundane world closer together. "I know you," the condemned say to him, and in one of the poem's most arresting moments a fellow Florentine rises from his sepulcher and calls to the poet because of the Tuscan accent in Dante's speech. The first great poet-theorist of the vernacular is detained for the length of a canto by a character nostalgic for his native speech. The tie between the temporal and the eternal could not be more firmly made. Virgil intrudes, cautioning Dante as he pushes him toward the open sepulcher, "Your words must be appropriate"—reminding the poet explicitly of what his role as guide and master always implies, that the journey proceeds by language and poetry.

It is hard to imagine anything more difficult than translating Dante. The language is distant and its nuances difficult, and the range of feeling and perception is enormous. Dante's verse simply cannot be replicated in English. We can fashion the three-line rhyme scheme but will lose the polysyllabic, feminine rhymes to accented monosyllables, or fall to low comedy. The abundance of rhyming words in Italian and their relative scarcity in English inevitably exchange fluidity for stilted mannerism. Allen Mandelbaum's new translation, *The Divine Comedy of Dante Alighieri: Inferno* the first volume of the California Dante, is done in unrhymed three-line stanzas. Mandelbaum's choice was clearly to concentrate on replicating the quickness and clarity of Dante's verse. Fortunately, the result is not at all slack or prosaic. By using techniques common to some contemporary poetry, Mandelbaum concentrates on the spoken rhythm of the lines. He follows the Italian (printed on facing pages) nearly line for line and traces poetic devices in the original.

The real concentration in Mandelbaum, as in Charles Singleton's prose translation, is on the faithful presentation of the poem's imagery. Some of Dante's fiercest partisans will choose the Singleton because they would rather not have the verse attempted at all. For the moment, I prefer the Mandelbaum for the compression and sense of discovery that even his open verse form provides. This is an exciting, vivid *Inferno* by a translator whose scholarship is impeccable. Mandelbaum has translated Ungaretti and Montale, and his translation of Virgil's *Aeneid* won the National Book Award in 1973. The work on Virgil was done while he was translating Dante and can be seen as part of the study for his work on the *Comedy*.

Mandelbaum's translations of the *Purgatorio* and the *Paradiso* will appear later this year in the same format, the Italian and English texts on large, facing pages set in elegant Monotype Dante with illustrations by Barry Moser. Eventually there will be three companion volumes of commentary. Moser's drawings are interesting for their clear debt to concentration-camp art and documentary photographs, both in imagery and in tone. Nearly all are character studies from specific passages in the poem. The Holocaust allusion adds a fierce contemporary dimension to the book, a reminder of another temporal Hell.

# IV

PART FOUR

18

## As Nightmare or Fancy:

## Trotsky Revisited

In 1902, at the age of 22, Leon Trotsky arrived in London and presented himself late one night on Lenin's doorstep as "The Pen." It was a codename settled on by one of Lenin's associates in the revolutionary newspaper, *The Spark*, who had helped Trotsky in his escape from Russia and had recommended Trotsky to Lenin as a writer for the paper. The name was used only for that occasion, but it might serve to describe much of Trotsky's life.

He was by profession and by disposition a writer. He had published his first newspaper at the age of 17; he picked up his first professional writing assignments along the train route to his first Siberian exile at 20. Despite his electric public role in 1917 and his governmental station in the first Soviet regime, he would always return most naturally to the pen. It was a reflex he would never lose, and it is a crucial part of what made Trotsky the complex figure he was, part of what made him in his final exile a figure of such dangerous and compelling energies, for Trotsky was the embodiment of the real political dangers of the writer-thinker; he had for two or three brief periods in his life translated what he wrote and thought into action.

Joel Carmichael's *Trotsky: An Appreciation of His Life* is a substantial political biography, which only occasionally is involved in the personal, psychological speculation we have grown accustomed to in contemporary biography. There is some concern for motivation throughout but only in dealing with Trotsky's inability to cope politically with Stalin's attacks on him are his interests in Trotsky's personality really focused.

In this section Carmichael raises an essential question: How was it that Trotsky, who had been so effective in 1905 as the leader of the first St. Petersburg Soviet and as the prime mover of the *putsch* of October 1917, was so successfully outflanked by Stalin? Carmichael offers, quite appropriately, a series of answers. Trotsky, who could galvanize masses of people at a public meeting, was never able to create a faction within the Party. In all the years after the Founding Congress of 1903 Trotsky played an independent role between the Bolsheviks and the Mensheviks; it was not until the late summer of 1917 that Trotsky was officially a Bolshevik, a designation that was almost coincident with his assuming leadership of public events in the capital.

Stalin, on the other hand, had always functioned with the Bolshevik organization; he was known as a "practical," an organizer. Carmichael's speculations on Trotsky's personality deal with his inability at the face-to-face party organizing that creates and holds factions, with his "shyness," and with a reluctance to assume full authority when it was offered, as it was several times. The shyness is attributed in part to Trotsky's uneasiness with his Jewish origins and in part to his relationship with his father.

Carmichael reasons that Trotsky's early rejection of his family and his cultural origins kept him from establishing an ego sufficient to accepting himself as a leader; specifically, "Trotsky's rejection of his father made it impossible for him to become a father in his own turn: he remained a son—a lost boy." For Carmichael, this was the source for the "lack of inner composure" that kept him from endearing himself to the other members of the Party after the

Revolution, and it was this that created both the years of contention with Lenin before 1917 and his lionization of Lenin after Lenin's death, in 1924.

This is shaky ground, and Carmichael quickly adds that any attempt at an extended psychoanalysis of Trotsky is impossible because there is so little intimate material available. The analysis seems inadequate to me and somewhat facile. Still, it is this attention to flaws in Trotsky that sets Carmichael apart from earlier writers on Trotsky, and the possibility of such questioning signals, perhaps, a new kind of discussion of Trotsky. Certainly, it was not a habit of mind accessible to Deutscher's thorough three-volume biography.

Carmichael is at his best, though, in describing political activity and is brilliant in his rapid accounting of the events of 1917. There his talent as a political writer and his Marxist sophistication combine to produce a highly energetic, and analytic presentation of events. I would recommend *Trotsky* for that chapter alone, though the book is strong and readable throughout.

The Victor Serge book is a curiosity in a number of ways. *The Life and Death of Leon Trotsky* was finished in 1947 and first published in France in 1951. It has original source material from Natalia Sedova, Trotsky's constant companion from 1903 to his death. It incorporates her diaries and accounts, presumably given in interviews with Serge in Mexico after Trotsky's death. It also incorporates Serge's firsthand experiences in Russia during the Revolution and with Trotsky in Europe after his banishment. The original materials here have been incorporated into Deutscher and Carmichael. What is strange about the book has more to do with events around it than with its contents, which are sometimes intimate (from Natalia) quite often cardboard (from Serge, especially his brief account of Trotsky's early life).

The dust cover of the book describes Serge as a Russian revolutionary novelist and an intimate of Trotsky in his Mexican exile. The first is true; the second is not. A few pages into the book you discover that Serge first visited the house at Coyoacan after Trotsky's death. Ah, well, just dust-jacketry. Not entirely, since the question of Serge's friendship was the subject of a bitter exchange in 1948 between Natalia and the *New York Times*.

The *Times* had quoted Serge's approval of Andre Malraux's Gaulist shift and associated that with a sense of Trotsky's approval, if he had lived. In that piece the *Times* identified Serge as a great friend of Trotsky in Mexico. Natalia replied, bitterly attacking Serge and indicating that the break between Trotsky and Serge was complete in 1939. At one point Serge was even implicated in the transport of the so-called "false will of Trotsky," which seemed to give credence to Stalinist charges against Trotsky as a counterrevolutionary. There is an extended account of this *Times* episode in Merleau-Ponty's book, *Signs*.

I bring it up as a matter of curiosity. How did this book come to be? The preface, by Serge's son, is of no help. The repetition in the dust jacket of the *Time's* claim for Serge's late friendship with Trotsky is the kind of thing that rekindles the sort of paranoia that is still a part of Trotsky's aura. The book is interesting, particularly in the quoted passages from Natalia Sedova. It springs, however, from such confusion that it is inevitably associated in my mind with the bitter and complex partisanship that surrounded Trotsky's exile and enclosed his supporters and his enemies for years after his assassination. It is a polarized particle, an ion somehow escaped from its own time. How it came into being, why it was published now are matters of speculation. Choose your own paranoia— political or commercial?

One of the early reviews of Carmichael's book talks about the demythologizing of Trotsky made possible by accurate, nonpartisan biography. If you take myth to mean only confusion, falsehood, and collective misunderstanding, then demythologizing is clearly possible and books—like Carmichael's—might have such an effect. But the mythic qualities of Trotsky are more important than that. At several levels Trotsky intersects—embodies, even—the shimmering ambiguities of modern politics.

Carmichael's approach to Trotsky, which does avoid collapsing into old Party arguments and manages to treat the man as both heroic and deeply flawed, does not dispel this energy but rather deepens it, offering it a substantiating range of detail. Let me raise a rather general question as illustrative of my point. How is a revolution, any revolution, to survive its own success? That is, how does the spirit of change survive the business of governing and all the consolidation it requires? It was a question that concerned Lenin as he neared his death and watched the early blooming of Soviet bureaucracy; it is what we feel, if only in our malaise, in the after-glow of the phantom revolution of the 1960s.

William Blake, in designing a mythology of political conflict, designated a father-ruler, who was overthrown by his son, who ruled in turn and was, in turn, therefore, despotic; but he also created a third figure, Orc, cloaked in fire, a spirit of perpetual change, who presides over a poem called, "America, A Prophecy." Trotsky's exile from Soviet Russia, his final residence in Mexico, the fact and the manner of his death all impel him toward Orc. The detailing in Carmichael of his inabilities as a party organizer, his aloofness, even his insecurities does not alter that direction; it merely explains it.

Trotsky's role in the Revolution of 1917 was *charismatic* (and I mean that in Max Weber's very specific sense, not in the sense the term is generally given in television newscasts). Reports from the scene describe his oratory, his voice, his lyricism, the emotional energy he gathered from and returned to the crowds he addressed. At one point in the July Days when the forces on the right had taken strength from revelations concerning the support the Bolsheviks had received from the Germans, Trotsky faced a hostile crowd of armed sailors. He was unable to stop their hostility with his speech and so reached down to touch a sailor's hand, as though the electricity might pass through his fingers to the sailor, from that one sailor to the entire crowd. The sailor would not touch him.

That moment seems more religious than political, or rather it takes its politics from a deep religious source. Later, more successfully, Trotsky avoided an armed assault on Petrograd's best protected military base by going in alone and talking the garrison into joining the Soviet.

It is as though all of Trotsky's work from his 17th year on had been validated. All the scrutiny and careful dialectical work found its rightness. The conjunction had a magic, a divinity to it, which Trotsky rode through October, 1917. When Lenin disembarked from "the sealed train" at the Finland Station, he had accepted Trotsky's 1906 formulation of "permanent revolution" as a way of dealing with the Marxist assumption that Russia would need a bourgeoise phase before it could have a proletarian phase—again, a rightness, a substantiation of Idea in the world.

Trotsky, the rationalist, seemed to accept his charismatic function. His basic impulses and his personality had always made him remote from organizational activity. The accession to his role in 1917 would make it impossible for him ever to return to organization. Accounts of his difficulties bear this out. Once his personal authority was questioned, it failed. Charismatic authority will not survive either doubt or mundane exercise. Orc changes; he does not rule.

There is more to the mythic Trotsky, I think, involving his role as a writer drawn to action. Even his inability to cope with Stalin in 1923–24 confirms something of our sense of the special qualities of the man of words and ideas. The heroic purity attributed to him by his followers in exile seems almost to rest on the border between theoretical justice and inaction.

He was an intellectual's touchstone. In some ways—and this was surely not his fault—he was the patron saint of their ineptitude. Left-wing intellectuals in the West were called upon to choose between Trotsky and Stalin, and John Dewey, the liberal American philosopher, went to Mexico and conducted a trial of Trotsky to counterbalance Stalin's Moscow charades. Dewey's sense of fair play was engaged here and his sense that the evidence would clear up the question. It did not. Evidence was not, finally, a part of the question. It was, I suspect, more a matter of affection and self-identification.

It wasn't until I was in college that I realized that Trotsky was not, in fact, still alive in Mexico, and that was fully seventeen or eighteen years after his death. For several years before that I believed from the vitality of the arguments that still raged about him that he was still there. Perhaps, in a strange way, he is. In an eastern Orthodox, a Russian, sense, an icon is never destroyed. At the moment the infidel's ax strikes the church wall, the sacred image recedes into it unharmed. Revolution is both a quotidian affair and a volatile modern Idea. In so far as Trotsky came to stand for the volatility of the Idea, he is inescapably a part of our dreams, as either nightmare or fancy.

## 19

## Revising Hitler

In 1934 Adolf Hitler consolidated his personal power over Germany by purging his own brownshirts of their independent, trouble-some leadership. The Night of the Long Knives, as the purge was called, claimed nearly 200 of the faithful, including Ernst Roehm, commander-in-chief of the SA and a Hitler supporter almost from the beginning. Hitler had been chancellor of Germany for just 18 months, but his control of the party and the country was so great that even this purge of Nazi notables caused almost no protest.

Within a month Hindenburg, President of the Republic, was dead, and Hitler assumed the joint title of chancellor and Fuhrer. In another month the first of the great Nuremberg rallies, the one Leni Riefenstahl named "The Triumph of the Will," was held. At the end of that year American visitors at the passion play at Oberammergau in different parts of the audience heard Germans exclaim, as Jesus was lifted onto the cross, "That is our Fuhrer, our Hitler!" When Judas was paid his 30 pieces of silver, many added, "That is Roehm." Hitler had captured more than political or military power; he had come to inhabit the minds of the people so completely that to think of it at any length is still frightening.

But we do think of it. In some peculiar way we even relish it.

John Toland's massive new biography of Hitler *Adolf Hitler* is just the most recent in a long series of biographical treatments, and Hitler is at the center of numerous memoirs and histories. There is an audience for Hitler and the Third Reich, one that relishes thick, heavily documented books with extensive photo sections.

Of course, the best of these books—and Toland's is no exception—contribute to the history of the period, but it is not historical interest that produces best sellers and book club selections; it is fascination, an unrelieved curiosity over the bonding political power, ruthlessness, military strength, and demonic energy that Hitler represents.

The bare facts of Hitler's life are well known, and his rise to political prominence in the beer halls of Munich has been extensively treated, as has his conduct of the war. Some early misconceptions persist, chiefly as folklore. He was never a housepainter or a paper-hanger. According to reliable medical reports, his sexual parts were normal. He probably didn't have a Jewish grandparent, though he clearly feared that he might have. Although he surely loved her, he was probably never comfortably intimate with his niece Geli, and he did not, as one movie has it, murder her or even have her murdered.

Much of what is true about Hitler makes him sound like a rather too eager contemporary. He was a frustrated artist and remained fascinated by artists and the arts all his life. He was taken with astrology but feared it, was a vegetarian, disliked drinking and hated cigarets so much that he forbade anyone to smoke in his presence. (He told Eva Braun she could give up smoking or stop seeing him and had Stalin's cigarette air-brushed out of photographs of the signing of the German-Soviet Pact.) He loved nature and rhapsodized over the countryside around the Berghoff, took long walks, hated urban congestion, liked dogs and children, loved music, thought hunting was an absurd practice and suggested to one hunter that he might just as well go to a slaughterhouse and watch cows being killed, and was an avid movie fan.

Thanks to a number of recent memoirs, a great deal is now known about Hitler's daily routine, his behavior with friends and associates, and his private life. Through a series of more than 250 interviews with Hitler's adjutants, his secretaries, his chauffeur, his pilot, his generals, interpreters, architects, and women friends he admired, John Toland expands the personal view of Hitler with a great deal of specific detail. There are some revelations. More characteristic of the book, though, is Toland's access to eyewitness accounts of Hitler's reactions to almost every significant event in his political career.

In his foreword Toland says that he set out to write his biography without a thesis, without any conclusions in mind. This is more than a polite nod to objectivity; Toland builds this biography from its smallest details outward. As reasonable as it sounds, this method is problematic, especially with a figure as complex as Hitler, a liar, posturer, play-actor, who was surrounded most of the time by people who had eagerly entangled their aspirations with his delusions.

Toland's method is particularly effective in presenting Hitler's early years. Hitler's life as a struggling artist in Vienna is especially vivid, as is Toland's treatment of Hitler's tour of duty in World War I. Oddly, Toland does not mention the trip Hitler made to England for five months in 1912–13, and there's no way of telling whether he doubts that the trip took place or thinks it unimportant. The omission stands out with a number of others throughout the book because the chapters here move month by month.

Toland is best at Hitler's early political career in Munich after the war. In this period the accumulation of anecdotal material gives a fine view of Hitler's development as a public speaker and his movement into the center of what was then the German Workers'

Party. The glimpses of Hitler's worn, ill-fitting suit and stained trenchcoat and the transformation he went through on stage from a comic figure to a hero are extremely valuable. Hitler was at his best with fractious, unruly crowds full of antagonistic leftists, and the material Toland has drawn together for this period heightens the sense of struggle and social chaos Hitler stepped into.

As Hitler becomes the center of German political life and is eventually enmeshed in international affairs, Toland's attention to minute detail and anecdote is less successful. Although he occasionally steps back to give a general view of the German social or economic climate, his tight focus on conference room exchanges and his subject's immediate reaction to every possible occurrence inevitably lets the general situation slip from view.

Toland's Hitler differs from the others we know in the degree of uncertainty ascribed to him. Throughout, Toland sees Hitler as a man torn by crisis, indecisive and anxiety ridden, and it is hard not to see this picture as a function of the biographer's method. His commitment to moment-by-moment reactions heightens the sense of confusion and inevitably reduces his sense of Hitler as the calculating manipulator of events.

Hitler's rhetoric is full of victims, both of persecution and of circumstance. Germany was the victim of Jews and Bolsheviks; it was the victim of the Armistice. He was a victim, Roehm's victim, the Communist's victim, the intended victim of phantom and real assassins. The Austrians were victims, so were the Sudeten Germans and the East Prussians. In his speeches Hitler portrayed himself as a man always driven to act, left without alternatives, and, obliquely, this is the view Toland accepts.

Toland's chapters dealing with the beginning of the war suffer from the same surfeit of detail. The center of the narrative is diplomatic. His exhaustive treatment of Hitler's talks with British Prime Minister Neville Chamberlain and his envoys and the fresh material presented on Axis relations are important and useful, but here, most dramatically, the sense of life in Germany and the careful preparation of the German people for war is lost, and pleadings by the general staff that the army is unprepared take the foreground along with Hitler's error in judgment concerning English and French reactions to the invasion of Poland. As much as Hitler may have tormented and wrangled, his original dates for the invasions of Czechoslovakia and Poland were the dates finally used.

In his brief account of the German people's anxiety over the beginning of hostilities, Toland ignores the militarization that had been developing in the country. A popular teachers' magazine from early 1938 offers lesson plans entirely devoted to warfare. Geography deals with troop dispositions in 1918. The most disconcerting section is the one on mathematics. One problem asks the angle to be used by a machine-gunner strafing a target at a specified distance. Another exercise has to do with the manner in which bombers can best avoid barrage balloons over London.

Hitler's attention to the "Jewish question," as it was called, had never failed him. By all accounts he had set it back in priority as he built his war machine and his alliances. It remained in his speeches and in his private conversations, though, an essential part of his world view. Exterminating the Jews was to be his legacy to the world, and he grew more feverish about the task as the war began to turn against him. At times he stressed the humanity with which it was all to be done. To anxious members of his inner circle who feared but obviously didn't want to know the worst, he explained that the final solution consisted merely of deporting Jews to the East. As things went badly in Russia, he wanted suffering as well as death for his ancient enemies, and he asked Heinrich Himmler if Jews couldn't be killed more appropriately as they were shipped East if the railroad car floors were drenched with quicklime. Himmler studied the proposal and replied that it was inefficient.

When asked about the slaughters in the Ukraine, Hitler said, "In the East I am concerned with space," and he went about making it. The sources for Hitler's deep anti-Semitism will probably never be fully known. Toland centers his attention on the Jewish physician who treated Hitler's mother for breast cancer with an exceptionally painful method. Though Hitler thanked the doctor profusely and even showed him some favors years later, Toland speculates that this episode may have wedded the Jew with pestilence in Hitler's mind. It should also be recalled that anti-Semitism was quite fashionable in Europe in Hitler's youth. In a 1921 letter describing his early career, Hitler said that "coming from a more or less cosmopolitan family I was anti-Semitic in less than a year."

Whether Hitler was insane, as some people still contend, is likely a false question. Toland avoids the psychopathology that has fascinated some commentators. Freud said he was mad. Jung said that Hitler's power was not political but magical. For Jung Hitler was a seer or a medicine man; his secret was that he allowed himself to be moved by his unconscious. This view is supported by much that we learn from Toland about Hitler in moments of decision. He would avoid information so as not to interrupt "the flow of intuition." Hitler's power over the German mind may have come, as Jung suggested, from the degree to which he shared its fears and humiliations and turned them out of his unconscious. What was eventually turned out upon the world and emulated was a torn, repressed psyche. Its hatreds and paranoias were given general orders, weapons, desperately thorough Eichmanns and Himmlers to handle the details and regiments for enforcement.

Toland's is a revised Hitler, made more ordinary by the weight of personal information by which he is surrounded, a somewhat humanized demon. But he is chilling still, both in his deeds and the way that millions of presumably civilized people shared his madness and in our curiously enduring, frightened attraction to him.

## 20

# Hitler Underground

Shortly after he became the German Chancellor, Hitler commissioned his architects to refurbish the Reich Chancellery. On an inspection tour with Albert Speer, then a young supervisor of construction, a door was discovered in the attic that opened onto a passageway through all the adjoining ministry buildings. The passage had been built during the Weimar Republic so that an earlier, beleaguered chancellor could escape the residence when it was surrounded by rioters. "Have the door walled up," Hitler said. "We don't need anything like that." What he needed in 1933 was a larger office and a "historic balcony" from which he could greet the crowds that came almost nightly to chant his name. Hitler was at the beginning of his most public phase, a period of mammoth rallies and thundering crowds, those monumental sculptures fashioned of searchlights and banners and phalanxes of uniformed party members. Twelve years later, in January 1945, after the collapse of the Ardennes offensive (the Battle of the Bulge), Hitler returned to Berlin from the West and moved his residence from the Chancellery to a concrete bunker buried in the garden. With the exception of two short automobile trips out of the city, occasional visits to his old office by means of a connecting tunnel, and rare nighttime walks with his dog in the garden, Hitler spent the last three months of his life in this cramped, unfinished bomb-shelter headquarters.

The bunker has been the center of a good deal of attention over the years. Myths and rumors about Hitler's death and a secret life in South America revolve around it, and the last-minute marriage to Eva Braun that was conducted there has given rise to its own area of speculation and fantasy. Most of the rumors were engendered by Stalin. News of Hitler's suicide reached him within a day after the event, and not long after the Russians captured the bunker they uncovered Hitler's and Braun's bodies in the garden. Positive identification came fairly quickly, but Stalin withheld the news, circulating, instead, stories that Hitler was alive and had been seen in various places around Europe. The Soviets had the bunker and all but a few of the eyewitnesses. Whether Stalin was holding back to build the perfect version so that his victory would be more complete or had a subtle plan involving epidemic paranoia among the Russians is hard to know. To counter these rumors, the British assigned to a young Oxford historian, Hugh Trevor-Roper, the task of investigating Hitler's death. With only a few witnesses available to him, he assembled an essentially accurate version of the last few days that was made public in November 1945. The uncertainty had had six months to germinate.

Even without the wilder Hitler lore, though, the bunker would have special qualities for the imagination. Hitler had built an image of himself that depended on large spaces—great halls, huge stadiums, and dramatic natural vistas. They were essential to the public view of Hitler and National Socialism that was circulated in photographs and newsreels. The idea of space—living space—was central to his rhetoric. Monuments and empire building were basic to his sense of statecraft. To the end he was fascinated by maps and architectural drawings. The manipulation of space was an obsession—one of many—with him. One particularly subtle propaganda photograph in a 1939 German women's magazine shows Hitler at the back of a large auditorium, alone in the last row of seats, his head tilted onto raised fingertips. His face is barely seen, but the head and hair are instantly recognizable. Rows of empty chairs stretch toward a distant podium, behind it the familiar, vertical Nazi banner. It is a graphic depiction of potential energy, a space about to be commanded by the master of such spaces.

The bunker is an imaginative retribution for this kind of power—for the rallies, banners, and screaming multitudes—Hitler without his crowds, isolated with a few dozen cronies, holed up, walled in, run to ground by day-and-night Allied bombing raids and two advancing armies. Hitler committed suicide to deny his enemies one last victory, the slow dismantling of his image that would have accompanied imprisonment and a trial. He wanted his body burned and the ashes hidden so that he and Eva might escape the humiliation that had already come to Mussolini. Although the cremation and secret burial were both inept, with Stalin's help he succeeded in keeping his image alive. However apt the bunker end may be, it has not discharged the energy that still surrounds Hitler. Movies are still being made, pulp magazines continue their dark fantasia of SS perversions, and major publishers continue their annual output of thick, expensive, quasi-scholarly Hitler books. There are three this season alone: a pictorial history by John Toland; an account of Hitler's war years; and John P. O'Donnell's *The Bunker*. The Third Reich is still good business.

O'Donnell is an American journalist who has worked in Germany since the war. As a U.S. intelligence officer in 1945 he was one of the first Americans to enter the bunker. The book begins with an account of that first visit, then turns to an account of Hitler's final stay below ground. This is not, however, a book focused on the day-by-day activities of the Fuhrer. He is seen frequently, of course, brooding, ranting, charting his own suicide, but O'Donnell is primarily interested in the bunker group, the people around Hitler at the end. More than a third of the book is devoted to events following the suicide, including a long description of the survivors' breakout and attempted escape to the Western Front. The book depends on a series of interviews with the survivors—members of the inner circle, secretaries, doctors, adjutants, and technicians; most appear on Toland's long list of interviewees in *Adolf Hitler* (1976). The interviews give O'Donnell's text some of the same questionable intimacy that characterizes Toland's work. This is a world made of bits and pieces, colored always by self-aggrandizement and self-justification and drawn frequently from the memories of minor players. These are the risks of history by reminiscence, but O'Donnell's style and his stammering organiza-tion magnify them. His tone throughout is a problem, always on the edge of tabloid sensationalism. It is also clear that he developed partisanships among his characters. When Hitler's chauffeur is sent along with Speer on a trip to the Western Front to keep track of Speer's activities, O'Donnell writes of the "moral sliminess of his stool pigeon mission." Speer's description of a brief period when he considered killing Hitler by putting a gas grenade in the bunker's ventilation system is counted as "the last of at least nine serious assassination attempts," although Speer never acquired the gas he wanted and the plan never proceeded past a few reconnoitering trips to the Chancellery garden. Even if Speer's account is taken at face value, O'Donnell's eagerness to add the episode to the von Stauffen-berg conspiracy as a serious attempt on Hitler's life betrays an overenthusiasm for discovery that calls many of the book's other assertions into question. The problem is deepened by the complete lack of documentation here—no list of interviews, no bibliography, no source citations. Except for occasional indications in the text itself, there is no way to distinguish what is taken from O'Donnell's original interviews from what comes from other books or mere folklore. It is a pity that the book took what I suppose could be kindly considered a popular form, both in tone and in the presentation of source material, because some of it is interesting and up to the general promise of the subject.

Bunker life was obviously a morose affair. The bombing could be heard from above and occasionally felt. Some of the bunker people held out for an escape to the Berghof in Obersalzberg. They were Hitler's "mountain people," whose best memories of the Third Reich were associated with that retreat. Time was passed in lengthy nostalgias. Some residents busied themselves with plotting to the very end. Martin Bormann schemed against his rivals in the bunker and elsewhere. In other parts of Germany, Himmler and Goering were both angling for power. No one there, except perhaps Hitler in his darkest moods, had any sense of how complete the Allied victory would be. The power brokers believed there would be a government after surrender to which they would be essential. There was also a brief drama over a leak in the bunker's security; details of Hitler commands found their way onto a British radio program, and Hitler wanted the leak stopped. O'Donnell constructs an elaborate and engaging story to explain the leak, involving a British spy, code-named Mata O'Hara, whom O'Donnell believes he has identified.

O'Donnell's journalistic method serves him best in his treatment of Hitler's suicide. He cross-interviewed the surviving witnesses, placing them all with reference to the event and checking their versions back, one against the other. Still, for all the vividness this makes possible, very little of importance is changed from the Trevor-Roper account of 1945. The first rendering had Hitler shoot himself through the mouth; O'Donnell says the bullet entered at the temple, and Trevor-Roper did not know that Hitler also bit a cyanide capsule at the same time that he pulled the trigger. O'Donnell brings the same kind of reporting to the Goebbels' suicides and to Magda's murdering of her six children. It is a chilling episode, even more so with the events at Jonestown so close at hand, one of those insane pieties, the Ph.D. propagandist and his Wagnerian wife dying in meticulous emulation of their leader, killing their children to foreclose the future as well. This is the bunker's finale, not the breakout of the survivors or the subsequent ironies—Russian women doctors arriving to sack Eva's bedroom of evening dresses and nylon stockings—but slaughter as an act of faith. While Hitler shuffled through the bunker for just over a hundred days, palsied and wasted by the drugs he was given by the charlatan doctor he trusted above all others, 500,000 additional people were executed in the death camps in the East as a part of the increased destruction he demanded when he knew the war was lost.

## 21

## Celine's Last Stand

Germany, 1945. The train on which he is riding stops beside the Kiel Canal. Louis-Ferdinand Celine, his wife Lili, their cat Bebert, and the 19 drooling, feeble-minded children they are escorting climb down from their flat car for a drink of water from a rainbarrel. They drink. A trainman lathers up by flashlight and lifts his razor to shave. A bomb explodes, and the trainman, barrel, and razor are all catapulted into the canal. More bombs. The children run off. Concussions lift the train and rattle it frantically.

Celine looks up and by the light of phosphorus flares from the bombers can see the retarded, deformed children pushing and shoving, laughing, playing tag on an iron bridge over the canal that bucks and snakes beneath them from the force of the explosions—a dance macabre, one of several as vividly seen, a *corps de ballet* to the *rigadoon* (a spirited dance for one couple) Celine and Lili perform as they cross and recross Germany as it collapses and explodes around them.

*Rigadoon* is Celine's last book, the final volume in the trilogy that includes *Castle to Castle* and *North*. Together they comprise a *chronicle* (Celine's word) of Celine's travels in Germany in 1944–1945, an excursion through the European apocalypse that all of Celine's work seemed to predict, a forced visit to a carnival of ruin and death for a man who had written to a friend in 1932, "I take pleasure only in the grotesque on the confines of death."

In 1944 Celine was practicing medicine in Paris. His place as a major modern French novelist had already been established by *Journey to the End of the Night* (1932) and *Death on the Installment Plan* (1936). Because of his collaboration with the Nazis, Celine's life was threatened by the Resistance, and he left France with his wife, their cat, and a friend and fellow collaborator, the movie actor La Vignan, intending to cross Germany and settle in Denmark.

The Germans confiscated his papers and refused to allow him to enter Denmark. Later, they refused his pleas to go into exile in Switzerland or return to France, and when he refused to broadcast Nazi propaganda, he was interned for three months in a Prussian prison camp (the setting for *North*).

Again he tried to reach Denmark via Rostok and Warnemunde, failed, headed south through Berlin and Ulm to Sigmaringen, near the Swiss border, where Vichy refugees were exiled. In March of 1945 he headed north again and finally reached Copenhagen.

*Rigadoon's* narrative begins in Rostok and follows the path of Celine's actual journey, though there are changes in sequence and the chronicle's clock is incredibly accelerated. This may not be a novel, but it is fiction of a special order that speeds along, driven by the energies of its only real characters, Celine the narrator (circa 1961) and Celine the refugee.

Before he begins the narrative in Rostok, we are treated to 30 pages of Celine vituperating—haranguing various friends, journalists, a would-be disciple, a spectral, long-dead associate, a neighbor. All of them get the same harsh treatment. In this prologue, which Celine with a backward glance calls "a homage to the reader," the writer presents himself as a man beset by fools and enemies; he drives them away. He also shows himself to be unregenerate—politically, racially, personally—convinced that his actions in the war were no worse than anyone else's, obsessed still with the mongrelization of the white race and the imminent arrival of the Chinese armies in France, angry at the betrayals of old friends and the inadequacies of favored writers.

However a sympathetic reader might want to come to Celine, he is stiff-armed along with one or another of these petitioners. We enter this incredible narrative without a hero, not even that heroic authorial sensibility that usually lurks behind the arras in most modern novels. There is just Celine, wizened and bitter chronicler of Europe's grandest *guignol*, egomaniacal and misanthropic.

It is this churlish voice—Celine, not Celine, the trilogy's fictive version of Celine (take your pick)—that makes the special brilliance of *Rigadoon* possible. What Celine has to offer is a world past insanity, an implosion of images so horrible and condemning that only the misanthrope could hold it in focus. Celine's style—the exclamatory, here almost screeching, tone, the wild collisions of diction, and his by-now-familiar broken, dot-riddled sentences— work perfectly, pressing the narrative on with great speed, casting up grotesque images sharply and quickly, making way frequently for Celine's obsessive refrains, and near the end of the book firing a weld between hallucination and reality of a kind that has just never been made before.

The result is a terrifying comedy, grotesqueries of matter, heaps of rubble, buildings that explode, people and cities adrift among fragments of incendiary phosphorus. Comic, still—a *Wehrmacht* field marshal dragged from his private railway car by a Berlin mob and hefted over the shoulders of a crowd that shouts "*Heil* . . . *schwein!*" The deaf general responds with smiles and little gestures of thanks as the shattered glass from the station's vaulted roof falls around them all like rain. In this setting every individual is funny, grostesque. Even Celine cuts a darkly comedic figure, walking painfully with the help of two white canes, a cruel dance.

It is a world unhinged; the lines of cause and effect have been fractured, and the only workable faith is suspicion, Celine's immense paranoia, which he leans on as completely as he does on his canes. Everything seems to float in fire or rubble, hilariously aligned or misaligned. When Celine is hit on the head by a flying brick in Hanover and begins to hallucinate, the hallucinations do not redeem or reconstruct; they deepen the horror in Hamburg, pressing the familiar ruins toward a vision of the final circle of Hell.

Despite the distance from which all of this stands to us and the ease with which the unregenerate Celine can be dismissed, *Rigadoon* speaks directly to the lives we are leading in American cities, places where the accepted level of terror and destruction is high enough to make what we call "a healthy paranoia" our best navigational aid. This is a brilliant book, superbly presented in English by Ralph Manheim, a study in the grotesque that plays back to our own grotesqueries—at least, to mine—in ways that can not easily be forgotten.

# V

PART FIVE

22

# A Commitment to Grit:

# Writing in Chicago

When the English poet Roy Fisher visited Chicago a few years ago, he had a list of things he wanted to see—the area on Halsted Street where Theodore Dreiser's Sister Carrie lived, the Board of Trade from Frank Norris's *The Pit*, Studs Lonigan's street corner on the South Side, the block on South Drexel where Bigger Thomas in Richard Wright's *Native Son* killed and incinerated his rich employer's daughter, Nelson Algren's Division Street, the train station where Louis Armstrong was met by King Oliver, and more. It was the kind of list that American tourists take to European cities, the product of a long and obviously vivid literary familiarity with Chicago. It was a reminder, as well, of the richness and variety of Chicago's literary past and an indication of the degree to which the city—its neighborhoods, streets, and buildings—is tangibly part of that heritage.

Dwelling at length on the literature of most major cities would involve a peculiar kind of travesty. Although New York is the unquestioned literary center of America, it would be strange to talk about the history of New York writing; the phrase almost immediately suggests something less than the whole, a literature specifically, even provincially, about New York. The notion of a London literature or a Paris literature verges on the comic. What makes

Chicago literature a subject worth extended attention as something other than Second City boosterism is the unique relationship that Chicago has had to the writing that has been done here. It makes the same kind of sense as Chicago architecture; like Chicago architecture, Chicago literature evolved with the city and because of it. It had distinct tendencies of style and content, related, certainly, to developments elsewhere in America and abroad but brought to a special cohesion here. This cohesion was facilitated by the fact that in much of the writing done here, Chicago was a subject, a part of the essential focus of the writer's attention.

Eventually, Chicago came to represent, almost mythically, a kind of reality. "Somber, heavy, growling, lowbrow Chicago," to use Saul Bellow's words, seemed to demand something of its writers, a commitment to a gritty, even brutal version of the world. "Just try to write in the classic tradition with that stink in your nostrils, sit down and spin out smooth poetic sentences"—this was Albert Halper's charge to himself as a young writer. It couldn't be done. The city whose very name had come to mean encroaching reality had its way. "If I was born in a raw slangy town, if I happened to see raw slangy things," Halper concluded, "why shouldn't my stuff be raw slangy?"

The literature that we identify with Chicago emerged in the 1890s as the city itself emerged as a metropolis. Of course, there were writers at work here before. The most notable were journalists— Eugene Field, Finley Peter Dunne, Opie Read, and George Ade— but the city had its share of versifiers, historical novelists, purveyors of romance, and a bustling trade in dime novels. It was a publishing center of sorts and provided a growing number of readers. Early on, there were signs of self-consciousness. Juliette Kinzie's *Wau-Bun* (1856), the first Chicago novel, is an account of the Fort Dearborn Massacre and her family's role in the founding of the city. A mixture of history, memoir, and fiction, the book is Chicago's first attempt at explaining itself. By 1880 the city had become a common setting for fiction. Thrillers and dime novels were frequently set in the more disreputable parts of the city. Shang Andrews's *Wicked Nell: A Gay Girl of the Town* (1877) follows the Moll Flanders-esque misadventures of a young prostitute who eventually repents, marries, and becomes a society matron. In the '80s, as well, fiction began to be used, without much literary distinction, as a means of arguing social issues. The Haymarket Square bombing in 1886 produced 15 novels, ranging from sensational thrillers to earnest fictionalizations that covered every conceivable explanation of the event.

Chicago's incredible growth in the period after the fire made it a center of international attention and a tourist attraction. Europeans visiting America were advised to see Niagara Falls, Yellowstone, and Chicago. The city was somehow pure American, the place where commerce, industry, population, and urban development ran wild. It was the center of economic power for the whole Midwest, the national trading center for grain and livestock; it was America's first wholly modern city, the home of the elevator and the skyscraper, the Oz that drew generations of young people away from small towns and farms, an El Dorado to immigrants, who came to Chicago in numbers that would shortly rival the populations of their own national capitals. Chicago was at once an aspiring cultural center intent on the arts and education and a rough, crude chaos of humanity at swirling odds with itself, "a Dis without a Dante," as one visitor called it. The city had already seen two bloody union battles, the National Railroad Strike in 1877 with 18 dead, and the Haymarket affair with 11 killed and hundreds injured. It had also weathered a number of bitter ethnic conflicts, including one between the Germans and the Irish that threatened for a time to break out into a full-scale war.

Somehow in this period Chicago hurried past one of the polite stages of urban development. It never successfully finished off the rough edges between political and economic power at their crudest and what is genteel and ceremonious in city life. Perhaps there wasn't time, or perhaps social veneer doesn't wear well in this climate. Whatever the cause, Chicago politics from Bathhouse John Coughlin to the present has been associated with boondoggles, deals, and "clout," the word that Chicago has given American English for the direct, shameless trading of influence. Although we owe the lakefront and the city's profile to such visionaries of the period as Daniel Burnham and Louis Sullivan, it could very well be argued that the patron saint of the Chicago style in entrepreneurship is Charles T. Yerkes, who built the el simply because he had run out of ground space to control and who got his plans for an underground railway downtown past the City Council by changing the dimensions on an ordinance permitting the installation of telephone cables while the legislation made the short trip from the council chamber to the city clerk's office.

Eventually, Chicago came to be known for its extremes, the objective extremes of growth and ethnic diversity, and for extremes of moral, social, and political corruption. In fact, Chicago was probably no more corrupt than any other major city of the period. Almost inevitably, the city that called attention to itself for monumental achievements of expansion would be known, as well, for its companion vices. Evangelists and reformers came to Chicago to meet the devil on his own ground, and so did social theorists and literary radicals. Subsequent Chicago history merely extended the image of corruption into a caricature. During Prohibition all large cities had gangsters; New York had great families of them, but only Chicago had Al Capone, the criminal celebrity in love with his own notoriety. Every large American city passed through a phase of machine politics with legendary political bosses, but only Chicago preserved it all as its principal political institution. In a familiar, if perverse, way Chicago's popular image at its most grotesque has become a matter of civic pride. The latter-day motto "The city that works" contains a justification of misdemeanor in favor of utility that Charles Yerkes could have been proud of. The city has not honored him with a street or a highway (he was driven out of town in 1890), but it clearly has never forgotten his way of doing business.

The Chicago renaissance in American literature, as the period from 1890 to 1920 is called, began, then, in a city that had achieved international prominence as a business center where capital had its own sway unchecked by political or social interference. Growth was the principal goal and wealth, great wealth, its conspicuous reward. Yerkes, for all his flourish, was a small-time entrepreneur compared with Swift, Armour, Field, Pullman, and McCormick.

American literary realism found a natural home in Chicago. The movement was then dominated theoretically and editorially by William Dean Howells, who had long had an affinity for local-color writing. Though its early uses had been patronizing and comic, realism argued for the value of the individual, rural, small-town experiences of the kinds of writers who gathered in Chicago. More important, realism's growing interest in social and economic determinism made the bustling new metropolis, with its undisguised lines of power, particularly useful. Under the influence of Emile Zola's idea of the novel as a laboratory for examining the environmental determinants of human behavior, realism became increasingly involved with the external forces that played upon the individual and less interested in the representations of national life proposed by Howells. In Chicago, external social forces were most blatantly represented by business and money.

Although the Chicago renaissance was given luster by the presence in the city of Hamlin Garland and Joseph Kirkland, two of the finest local-color writers of the period, the first novels in what would become the Chicago school of fiction were written by Henry Blake Fuller, a third-generation Chicago businessman and sometime aesthete. Fuller's two most successful books, *The Cliff-dwellers* (1893) and *With the Procession* (1895), contain the basic elements that would be developed by Chicago writers for decades, though Fuller was no environmental determinist and his harshest views of the city seem polite when compared with the much more critical urban realism of writers whose work followed quickly on his. Both of Fuller's novels focus on business. In *The Cliff-dwellers* he deals with the working lives of a group of businessmen whose offices are in the Clifton, a downtown Chicago office building. The Clifton allows Fuller to present a range of businessmen and business behavior. All are cliff dwellers because of the shape of their modest skyscraper; because of their businesses, all are primitives whose work keeps them from higher pursuits. Of the two books, *With the Procession* is the more tightly constructed and is richer in thematic development. The family treated in the novel resembles Fuller's own old Chicago family. David Marshall, the father, is an old-style businessman, out of step with the new Chicago. The newer element is represented by Belden, Marshall's partner, a "pushing fellow" Marshall took on at a point of crisis and could never shake off. Younger and more ambitious than Marshall, Belden is also "fundamentally insolent and selfish." The procession of the title is the glittering social procession of Chicago's new wealth, which Marshall's daughter desperately wants to join. Doing so destroys Marshall, and the rewards for his children are merely lassitude and funds enough for one daughter's escape to England and his son's trip to Japan.

Marshall's obituary is an account of his business life and a rehearsal of Chicago's early history, from Indian village to metropolis. His death marks the end of the old town, and the city passes into the hands of Belden and a class of similar opportunists. Although Fuller's critique of city life is essentially conservative, the introduction of the details of business life is important. In the movement of his own business out of his control and the shift in his dealings toward opportunism and marginal legality, Marshall is arguably the first in a long series of Chicago fictional characters whose lives pass out of their own control and into the hands of others because of the imperatives of commerce. Fuller himself devoted years of work to the "upward movement" in Chicago, which had as its goal the establishment of institutions that would elevate the city's spirit through art and education, but the representative of Fuller's aesthetic temperament in the novel, Truesdale Marshall, David's son, is little more than self-important. He is the spokesman for Fuller's distress at the appearance of the city and its squalid bustling, but he lacks the energy or conviction to change any of it.

The Chicago realists who followed Fuller, in particular Will Payne and Robert Herrick, concentrated their efforts on the negative aspects of the city. In Herrick's fiction the city functions as a palpable force against his characters. The limitations of the pervasive business mentality and the corrosive power of greed foreclose their aspirations and ideals. Though Herrick was attacked for the baseness and brutality of his novels, their principal characters are not lower class but middle class, drawn back from their best possibilities by the sheer force of the city. For Herrick the city was a moral blight, and he often turned his fine descriptive powers to the meanest, most blighted areas to confirm his judgment.

The most important book with a Chicago setting in this period, Theodore Dreiser's *Sister Carrie* (1900), opens on a train entering Chicago. Carrie Meeber, like similar figures in the works of Garland, Payne, and others, leaves small-town Wisconsin life for the city and its glimmering dream of success. The Chicago portion of *Sister Carrie* is brilliant in its depiction of the confining qualities of the sprawling city and wonderful in the sense that it provides of the city's workers. Carrie, whose mind is aswirl with bright things, finds her first job in a boot-polish factory.

What distinguishes Dreiser's work from that of his European predecessors is the naïve faith in will that Carrie sustains for so much of the book. She believes that the ideals of progress can apply to her, but they do not. She achieves some notoriety but no freedom, and eventually she only sits staring, rocking in a chair by the window, her dreams separated from her at some gray distance.

Chicago's function in the novel is crucial. The city was the point of access for the rural youngster to the new American life, and when Carrie first sights it from the train window she sees only its promise for her, not its crushing enormity. Walking later on Van Buren Street, looking for work, Carrie feels the "power and force" of the city but does not understand it. Its purposes are beyond her, and each step she takes gives her an increasing sense of helplessness. The contrast between her first views of the city as spectacle and her Van Buren Street attempt to deal with it, to use it, holds the core of Dreiser's sense of Chicago and his acute sense of the dilemma of his character. The spectacle of the city, the idea of progress and achievement given miraculous shape before her, encourage Carrie's dreams for her future; it is in its utilitarian mode that the city suggests her ultimate failure with the visible signs of "strange energies and huge interests" that she will never comprehend, let alone master. There is a relentlessness to Dreiser's working out of Carrie's defeat. She is neither saved nor destroyed. Dreiser is not equivocal about her ending, as some early critics charged, but precise. The finale of the dream of mobility is agitated stasis.

In *Sister Carrie* Dreiser deals with one aspect of the idea of Chicago. In two later novels he treats the other half of the contrast with which he opens *Carrie*. *The Financier* (1912) and *The Titan* (1914) both deal with the acquisition and manipulation of power, the force that lay behind those mysteries Carrie could not comprehend. Dreiser's central character for this series, a proposed "trilogy of desire," is Frank Cowperwood, a fictionalization of Charles T. Yerkes, the traction king.

Chicago's role in the national consciousness as the center of rampant capitalism is best seen in the work of two non-Chicagoans who used the city in their most polemical books, Upton Sinclair and Frank Norris. Sinclair's *The Jungle* (1906) vividly depicts the brutality of life in Chicago's packinghouses. Jurgis Rudkins, Sinclair's packinghouse worker, is dehumanized, transformed into a version of the product of his labor in the vilest, most unsanitary conditions. Although the immediate response to the novel focused on the industry's lack of sanitation, Sinclair had intended the story to be a case in point, an instance of business unchecked by regulations or the countervailing force of organized labor. Sinclair visited Chicago only briefly. Obviously the packing industry drew him as a subject, but he was also taking advantage of the place that Chicago held in the American mind.

Frank Norris was born in Chicago, but his literary career is almost entirely identified with San Francisco. Norris lived here for a few months while he did research for his most ambitious work, *The Epic of Wheat*, a trilogy that he did not live to complete. Two volumes, *The Octopus* (1901) and *The Pit* (1903), were finished; the third, to have been called *The Wolf*, was never begun. In these novels Norris set out to document the relationship of capital and speculation to human life. The octopus of the first novel is a monstrous configuration of the country's system of pricing, selling, and distributing wheat. The monster's head is Chicago's Board of Trade; its tentacles extend across the whole country, into every Kansas farm, through the rail lines, and outward again to every point of distribution. *The Pit*, subtitled *A Story of Chicago*, deals specifically with the Board of Trade and its workings. The pit, then as now, is the trading floor of the exchange.

A short sketch for the trilogy can be seen in Norris's story "A Deal in Wheat" (1903), in which two brokers vie for control of the market. As a result of their competition, the story's main character, Sam Lewiston, is driven from his Kansas farm and forced to look for work in Chicago. In one of Norris's bitterest ironies we see Lewiston waiting for a midnight handout in a Chicago bread line, only to be turned away because the depressed price of wheat that drove him to the city in the first place has been manipulated upward. The bakery can no longer afford its charity.

In the final chapter of *The Pit*, after the Board of Trade has done its destructive work on the novel's characters and their families, the building is seen from the rear window of a carriage, "black, monolithic, crouching on its foundation like a monstrous sphinx with blind eyes, silent, grave." In Norris, as in Sinclair, those forces that Carrie saw on her morning walk are figured forth as monsters or beasts. They are created by men but are out of men's control. Both of these novelists take the idea of Chicago in fiction to its logical extreme. Their powerful use of the popular image of the city provided the model for naturalistic and proletarian novels for three decades.

The drift of Chicago realism is clear in Dreiser, Sinclair, Norris, and the writers who followed them and, in retrospect, implicit in their Chicago renaissance predecessors as well. Realism was not a passive reflection of reality but an active imposition of social and political values. In its earliest, local-color phase it argued for the value of native experience. By the turn of the century in Chicago, it had become the fictional mode for homegrown American socialism. Outraged, naïve, often prone to simplistic, heavy-handed ironies, realism had its roots in Midwestern populist distrust of urban politics and money. It was also attached to old strains of American idealism. Chicago realism would eventually provide a lively precedent for the novels of Floyd Dell, Albert Halper, James T. Farrell, Richard Wright, and Nelson Algren.

The idealism in all of this was based on simple democratic principles—the idea of brotherhood as an outcome of equality, a positive sense of the salutary influence of the land on its people, the value of direct labor. Early in the history of the Republic, euphoric enthusiasms for equality led to pots, bowls, dishes, silverware, all the same size—an effort, it would seem, to extend political ideas into the tangible world of made things with all the seriousness of liturgical consistency. This idealism was always implicit even in the darkest tales of the realist tradition. If the perfection of *Homo americanus* seemed to be a less immediate possibility than it once had been, there was still a spirit of reform in nearly all the work of the Chicago school. Giving direct voice to this idealism was the chore of the three most important poets associated with the movement, Edgar Lee Masters, Carl Sandburg, and Vachel Lindsay. All three came from rural Midwestern backgrounds. Masters and Sandburg were both raised on the ebullient socialism of Robert Ingersoll, as was the novelist and editor Floyd Dell.

Some of Masters's poems before *Spoon River* are directly political. Others argue the need for personal freedom through self-fulfillment, a modern-dress version of a familiar ideal. In *Spoon River* Masters gives secret voices to the people of his town. To some extent this serves to expose the flaws and hypocrisies of the citizenry. The method is realistic, and some of his speakers are caught in the familiar realistic dilemma, like the butcher who sees himself crushed between Governor Altgeld and Philip Armour, between political and economic forces. The effects of realism's methods and some of its favored conflicts are different in Masters's poems from what appears in fictional prose about the same subjects. The poems ennoble their speakers, even in their meanness, or, in the case of the butcher, in his confusion. Finally, the butcher lets the blame slide back on himself: "Who was it/Armour, Altgeld or myself/That ruined me?" The effect is of ingratiating candor, not irony. The ironies that moved in modernist poems of the same period, the oblique monologues of T. S. Eliot and Ezra Pound or the more direct speeches of Edwin Arlington Robinson's poetry, were simply not part of Master's poetic arsenal. Whatever his initial intent, the final effect of the *Spoon River* poems is one of positive individualism.

Populist idealism is essential to Sandburg's work. Assessing the sins of Chicago, the city so reviled for its destructive capabilities for so long, he faults it primarily for coaxing so many youths away from the vitalizing dew of their native farms. In the middle of the famous poem "Chicago," Sandburg lists the city's faults, and the list reads like a realist's bill of particulars. His answer is that energy, "coarse and strong and cunning," overrides the city's admitted horrors. In the end a high-school mural of rough, simultaneous, though not collective, labor overcomes all objections, despite the personal witness given in the "I have seen"s and "Yes, it is true"s of the middle of the poem. The desire for rhapsodic affirmation in Sandburg sometimes reaches the level of desperation. "Chicago" illustrates, as well as any single Sandburg poem, what is most winning and most limiting in his work.

By 1920, when the Chicago renaissance is said to have ended, all the elements of the Chicago novel and the Chicago poem had been developed. This literature was very different from the modernism being practiced by expatriate Americans in Europe. The characteristic fragmentations of modernism, its quick, nervous, invented forms, have almost no place in the Chicago school. The differences were most graphically seen in the mixed list of contributors and occasional conflicts in Chicago's two great literary magazines, Harriet Monroe's *Poetry* and Margaret Anderson's *Little Review*. In true Chicago spirit Harriet Monroe adopted the slogan "To have

great poets you must have great audiences." Ezra Pound, her
foreign correspondent, was irate. Poets, he insisted, have nothing to
do with audiences. Nothing could have more clearly marked the
differences between them. Still, Monroe kept an open door and in
the period of her editorship published the most impressive list of
contributors ever accumulated by a magazine, including poets of the
Chicago group, as well as the modernists. The same mixture, but
broadened to include fiction and general criticism, can be seen in the
Chicago years of *The Little Review*.

Novels and stories in the Chicago style with Chicago settings
continued to appear throughout the 1920s, and the mode had a
genuine revival in the 1930s because of the political interests roused
by the Depression. But most of what appeared lacked distinction.
The novel that revived the form and gave it an entirely new life was
James T. Farrell's *Studs Lonigan: A Trilogy* (1932, 1934, 1935). The
three volumes, *Young Lonigan, The Young Manhood of Studs Lonigan*,
and *Judgment Day*, cover 15 years in the life of an Irish boy on the
South Side, from age 14 to his death at 29.

    *Studs Lonigan* is an effort to set down an American life completely,
to show the evolution of attitudes and behaviors with complete
candor. The result is a novel that is sometimes lyrical but more often
brutal. Farrell's intent was consciously realistic. In discussing the
book, and in the defense he was required to make at the censorship
trial it provoked 16 years after its publication, Farrell always used
the terminology of naturalism and realism. The book's language
was taken from life, he said, and its episodes were all verifiable in his
own experience as a young man in Chicago. Farrell's associations
with the Chicago tradition in fiction were firm. The first version of
Studs's story was submitted to James Weber Linn, his writing
teacher at the University of Chicago. It was also read by Robert
Morss Lovett at the university. Both men had been early colleagues

of Robert Herrick's, and both men were novelists of the early Chicago school.

*Studs Lonigan* is, for all its convenient associations, not typical of the school. Studs is not a deprived proletarian; his father is a successful plasterer who owns a car and boasts a substantial bank account. Though Studs is clearly trapped, he is caught by the forces of his own immediate culture and the neighborhood values it fosters. Great economic patterns have very little importance in the book, and the city's role as the engine of business power is not developed here. On the contrary, one of Farrell's persistent ironies in the sequence, one that follows Studs almost to the point of his death, is that the city offers opportunities for learning, for political and cultural awareness that might have spared Studs his failures and his early death. The pertinent world for Studs Lonigan is not the city but the neighborhood, and in three volumes he rarely ventures out of it. In Farrell's work, the city is not abstracted into a single force or contrived into a metaphoric monster; it is immediate and concrete, the neighborhood with all of its sidewalks, fences, telephone poles, and fireplugs firmly, almost luminously, in place.

Studs's entrapment is the work of the lower-middle-class Irish culture around him and of the limited, though hugely satisfying, alternative he finds for it in a 58th Street gang. The culture of the street corner, with its studied cynicisms and meticulous posturings, provides Studs with nearly all of the best moments in his life. Others escape into versions of adulthood. Studs always drifts back. At one of the low points in his dissipation we see him draped over the same fireplug he played around as Lone Wolf Lonigan at the age of 14. The street corner's alternative, which seems in its sass and strut to be an extreme one, is for Farrell just a more clamorous complacency, and Studs Lonigan is its archacolyte. One of the continuing charms of young Lonigan is that for most of us Studs is an intensely familiar character. If you had an urban youth, you invariably had a Studs Lonigan, a street-corner hero whose life peaked at 16 or 17 within six or eight square blocks of mythic identity. Drive through the neighborhoods today and you can see versions of Studs in the making; stop at neighborhood coffee shops on Saturday morning and you can see what's left of them after a few years.

*Studs Lonigan* is a trilogy about fragmentation. Paddy Lonigan, Studs's father, opens the sequence with nostalgia about his own boyhood. After his son's early death, he goes to his old neighborhood on South Archer to commemorate his own lost youth, and in doing so, offers an appropriate memorial to his son. In a culture that provides no real, continuous steps into adulthood, the society of boyhood and the street takes on an exaggerated importance. To escape, as Danny O'Neill did in Farrell's other long sequence of novels or as Farrell himself did, requires a repudiation of the values of the street corner in favor of those of the despised seriousness of adult life. In its affection for detail (no other Chicago novel presents the city with such accuracy) and in the almost incantatory use of names throughout, *Studs Lonigan* is curiously elegiac. Beneath Farrell's well-reasoned critique of the lower-middle-class Irish culture that surrounds Studs and participates in his destruction, there is an affectionate sense of loss. To this extent at least, *Studs Lonigan* is an urban pastoral, the first of many. Whether used consciously or unconsciously, it is the informing spirit behind a host of stories, novels, and movies about urban American male adolescence, from Farrell's day to *Mean Streets, Saturday Night Fever,* and *Diner.*

Perhaps the most powerful book in the Chicago tradition in fiction is the one that most clearly supersedes it. Richard Wright's *Native Son* has about it many of the characteristics noted from the first in Chicago realism. The book's principal character, Bigger Thomas, is once again an individual caught by the forces of a larger society that he does not fully comprehend. In the contrast between Thomas's background in the ghetto and the life of the Daltons, the rich family that hires him, there is that familiar cross-play of social levels seen in earlier Chicago novels. But there is a difference and a substantial one. It has to do with race, but not solely. For both Farrell and Dreiser, the novel was a laboratory in which life was observed. Carrie is observed, and, despite the closer range, so is Studs. The question of identity in *Native Son* is more complex because the novel is at once realistic, subtly allegorical, and intricately ironic.

The setting of *Native Son* is a familiar, verifiable Chicago, with its streets and houses properly laid out. The psychological topography of the book has quite another shape, though it occupies the same terrain. To avoid being suspected of a racial transgression, Bigger Thomas accidentally commits a murder, and from that moment on he exists in another world of fear and its monstrous possibilities, a vertical world in which every path is a descent, one in which the escape from stereotype is its fulfillment. In the terrified moments in Mary Dalton's bedroom, Bigger Thomas passes into a proximity with one of the powerful centers of racial fear and hatred and is irrevocably impelled toward it. Later in the novel he murders again, and the second murder cannot be excused as an accident.

In the final section of the novel, which deals with Bigger's incarceration and trial, Bigger must find himself among the consequences of his actions. He is offered a full-blown social interpretation of what has happened to him by the radical supporters of his defense. Bigger's rejection of this reading of his story puts a curious turn in the novel. Finally, he has to take control and wrest himself away from what we might want to make of him. The whole tragedy, after all, was begun not by a segregationist but by Mary Dalton's naïve radicalism and the well-meaning enthusiasms for Negroes among her white, Leftist friends, members of the class that made up Wright's first readership. The novel turns on its readers and their practiced explanations of social problems. It even confronts Wright himself, because his success was built on that liberal-minded audience. Bigger, who had emerged slowly— from "Big Boy," an early story, and from Wright's own autobiography—is a character in whom Wright himself is implicated. Wright was a long-time member of the Communist Party, and Bigger's rejection is related to Wright's own ambiguous departure. To give this connection additional firmness, Mary Dalton takes her name from a New York party official who was sent to Chicago in the thirties.

In its concern for identity and in the objective power that it gives the demonic, *Native Son* exceeds its realistic backgrounds and is most comfortably read in the company of the works of Dostoyevsky, Sartre, and Camus or with Ralph Ellison's *Invisible Man*, which despite its greater stylistic range and pyrotechnic skill would be unimaginable without *Native Son*'s example. Although some reviewers compared *Native Son* with *An American Tragedy*, neither Farrell nor Dreiser produced a novel as complex as *Native Son*. Still, Chicago, the literary place where unresolved social conflict and the immediate juxtaposition of wealth and poverty have an unquestioned reality, is made use of in the novel.

In his sense of the demonic effects of race and their tragic implications, Cyrus Colter is very close to Wright. Colter, who had a long career as an attorney and a public official in Chicago, didn't begin publishing until late in life, but he and Wright are contemporaries and can be very usefully read together. The central characters of Colter's three novels—*The Rivers of Eros, The Hippodrome,* and *Night Studies*—are people who attempt to control their own lives. Clotilda Pilgrim in *The Rivers of Eros* has a sin in her past that, despite the fervent order and dignity she has willed into her life, works its way out not as she suspects—through some flaw in the granddaughter she loves and ultimately destroys—but as a by-product of the force of will she applies to suppress it. In *The*

*Hippodrome* Colter's protagonist has killed his wife and carries her head with him through the city. Like Bigger, he thinks that the monstrous act he has committed has freed and empowered him. In fact, it entraps him. He has killed his wife because of her sexual involvement with her white employer and as a result falls under the control of the proprietress of the Hippodrome, a ghetto sex show with black performers and white spectators. Still, he thinks that he is in control, that he can rule his life by ending it. But the sexual furies that derided Clotilda to the point of madness—and that with more complex range inform the compulsions of *Night Studies*—are in full flight here. He doesn't die; he performs wildly, tirelessly. Bigger Thomas ends with an assertion that what he did must have meant something. In *The Hippodrome* the meaning is acted out in front of a delighted white audience, representatives of that race whose need for purity had wished its own sexual furies onto blacks in the first place.

The figurative power of *The Hippodrome* and its movement toward myth are balanced in Colter's work by the variety of life presented in his short stories and his other two novels. The realist in Colter gives us a range of characters and interests rarely seen in treatments of black Chicago. Clotilda's boarders offer a concise view of this variety; *Night Studies*, with its added spectrum of social and economic class, documents it.

Nelson Algren may have been the last great writer of the Chicago school. There is a commitment to grit in Algren, an argument, often implicit but nevertheless there, that a working, even walking, knowledge of the lower end of the social spectrum is the only fit pursuit of reality. So he became a card player, a horse player, a savant of the lower depths. It was not his world, not a birthright in the way that the South Side was to Farrell or the West Side was to Albert Halper or Meyer Levin, but a métier, a world he chose as his subject matter in exchange for his own proletarian background.

Unlike other urban writers, Algren did not escape the world he wrote about but situated himself, until he left for New Jersey later in life, in its midst. And when he did leave, there was a sense that Chicago had failed him, that like Huck's Hannibal it had begun to smack of Sunday school; so he lit out for the territories, for Paterson and a new purity, a story—Rubin "Hurricane" Carter's murder trial—with all the elements of his inverted realism intact.

Stylistically, Algren is always a poet, sustaining his vision in a swirl of language, waiting—sometimes impatiently—for his narrative to cross paths with a moment suited to his own brand of rhapsody. He has the finest sense of sheer chaos of any American writer since Stephen Crane, those moments when everything simply and miraculously goes to hell. In both the short stories and the novels, these are his best scenes—when everything bounces out of place and then is held in suspended disarray while the novelist deliciously, comically describes it. The brutal barroom brawl near the end of A Walk on the Wild Side works this way, as does the wonderfully funny episode with the coffeepot, the yellow shoes, and the mosquito, where the combined momentums of sex, business, and personal style are knotted together from several meandering elements of the novel's plot. "Grind, grind, you coffee grinding man," says the ecstatic woman Dove is making love to as he tries desperately to reach the sample coffeepot he hopes to sell her, to retrieve his shoes, and to withstand the drilling of the mosquito on his exposed backside. It is this same finely tuned sense of disorder that gives Frankie Machine's dilemma its dark comedy in The Man with the Golden Arm and that enlivens Bruno Bicek's dismal fall in Never Come Morning.

The cast of characters in Algren is arguably real. If you doubted it, he would certainly have been capable of giving you a tour of that city that would have included people of his acquaintance who more than matched the bizarre qualities of Bruno, Frankie, Molly O.,

Blind Piggy, and Nifty Louis. They are all citizens of what he called
"the nation of furnished rooms," genuine because they are too far
gone not to be. They do not have any of the typicality that realism
and naturalism required. Algren's stories are not dramas of the
individual caught in an indifferent, mechanistic society. His characters are, to invoke his own voice, *characters*, plausible grotesques.
There is no Everyman here inviting allegorical interpretation, and
although Algren had a long history with the Left, there is little in the
way of direct political intent. Rather, there is the conviction that
among the extremes of character and human behavior you can find
the inevitabilities of the heart in all their terrifying beauty. Chicago
served Algren because it gave him the figures of his dark romance
and patined them, as it always has in fiction, with a sense of reality.

Saul Bellow has always posed a problem for the chroniclers of
Chicago's literature. The work of the city's most distinguished and
most honored writer doesn't fit any of the models for Chicago
fiction, nor does it, except in the social speculations of one section
of *The Dean's December*, treat Chicago as its subject. All this could
be taken as a sign of Bellow's place as a truly major figure; he simply
defines himself. But there is more to it, certainly. In large measure,
Bellow has helped to move the interests of American fiction away
from a concern with the effects of environment and toward an
interior struggle for identity and a firm, if usually momentary,
attachment to some confirming reality in the outside world. In its
fervent quarrel with the way things are, realism held onto a naïve
sense of conviction not only in change but also in things themselves.

The predicaments of Wilhelm, Herzog, and Citrine are dilemmas
of consciousness configured only incidentally as ambition or desire.
*Seize the Day* ends with a failure in commodities trading, but that
defeat does not put us back in the familiar territory of the individual
caught by external economic forces. Wilhelm seeks out the market
as a potential confirmation of personal value. It is a plaintive gesture

by a failing individual. Having lost out with everything close at hand, he asks for a sign from an external system of values.

Bellow's later characters are even more distinctive for the weight and complexity of the intellectual baggage they carry to their experiences. There is no explanation of Herzog's actions that is not already in his great census of explanations. Like Citrine in *Humboldt's Gift*, he is exhausted with explanations. Post-Freudian, postrevolutionary, postexistential, Bellow's characters testify to the irreducible quality of the problems they face.

The backgrounds of Bellow's work are largely European, and his intellectual agility gives the novels a range of reference and allusion reminiscent of high modernism. His maintenance of a traditional novelistic form against modernism's movement toward formal experimentation serves only to make the line of struggle more acute. It is a coincidence, but a propitious one, that the novelist whose work defines the postwar American novel's virtuoso skill at internal torment should be a citizen of Chicago, where fiction developed its longest attachment to the external. Still, Bellow is not placeless, as some of the critics who concentrate on him as an exemplar of the Jewish writer make him. Chicago has a special role in the landscape of Bellow's novels. The city is the setting for *Dangling Man* and the starting point for *The Adventures of Augie March*, but it is also a strange kind of test—quixotic, unpredictable, and humorous. When Herzog comes to Chicago, he falls into a labyrinth, with its streets consciously bent out of their usual shape, and he crashes, a Daedalus fallen back into his maze. Citrine's Chicago visit is masterfully comic. Citrine the explainer, the dedicated purveyor of ambiguities, is offered an old-style Chicago explanation of the way things are by a gangster, a representative of Chicago's popular myth. The essay section of *The Dean's December* that deals with Chicago was apparently first written for a book on the city that would be a companion to Bellow's book on Jerusalem.

The polemic is more curious and quirky than profound, with Winston Moore, the former head of the Cook County Jail, presented as a contemporary hero. As oddly as the section sits in that novel, it found, I think the right kind of home. It is an extrapolation of contemporary urban distress, a fiction of its own special sort, not the measured assessment that the companion to *To Jerusalem and Back* would have required. Perhaps Bellow's relationship with Chicago, actually and imaginatively, is still too active to be codified.

Contemporary Chicago writing is a reflection of the diversity of American writing in general. Certainly the old realistic aegis has no real contemporary force except in late-night barroom nostalgias. But then, there has always been more variety than I have noted here. I have been following one thread, and certainly there are others. The most sternly classical vein in recent American poetry, to cite just one example, had its beginnings in the Poetry Club at the University of Chicago in the 1920s, with Yvor Winters, Janet Lewis, and others. Other modes of fiction were written in and about Chicago, always. Much of the unfinished business of Chicago realism has become the province of Studs Terkel's oral histories. They are moved by the same faith in the individual, by common language, and by a clear belief that in the stories of ordinary people we can find both understanding and purpose. In one sense, and not an entirely flippant one, Terkel's tape recorder and that profound sense of sympathy he also carries with him are the inheritors of the Chicago school.

A number of fine novelists live and work in Chicago. Sometimes their work has a Chicago setting; often not. The one most easily identified with the Chicago school of writing is Harry Mark Petrakis, whose earlier accounts of Greek life in the city are based, like much ethnic literature, on realistic models; his later work has a much more lyric quality. Richard Stern's considerable achievements are often locally overshadowed by his proximity at the University of Chicago to Saul Bellow and the number of interests that their works have in common. From *Golk* through *Natural Shocks*, Stern has written fiction of remarkable clarity and stylistic strength, and his essays, especially "The Books in Fred Hampton's Apartment," are among the best prose pieces written on contemporary American life. The most dazzling version of Chicago in fiction in the past few decades is to be found in the novels of Leon Forrest. A magical realist with antecedents in Faulkner, Ellison, and a number of contemporary Latin American writers, Forrest has created out of the lyricisms of black speech and Baptist pulpit oratory a phantasm of the South Side. *The Bloodworth Orphans* is one of the most original books produced in contemporary America, a riffing account of incest, evangelism, hoodoo, and transfiguration. Its language moves with the speed and nervous energy of bebop. Like Gabriel Garcia Márquez and Charlie Parker, Forrest leaves you with the strange sense that pure invention is the only reasonable approach to reality. Though he gives us a version of Chicago that is completely persuasive, he is as far from the Chicago school as it is possible to be.

Poetry has flourished in Chicago in recent years. For a long time this was a city where some poets happened to live, among them Kenneth Rexroth, Allen Tate, Yvor Winters, Hayden Carruth, David Waggoner, Karl Shapiro, Isabella Gardner, and John Nims. In the early 1960s John Logan taught a poetry workshop in a downtown office that produced some of the most interesting poets writing today; Marvin Bell, Dennis Schmitz, William Hunt, Charles Simic, Bill Knott, and others, though now working in other places, acknowledge their beginnings in that workshop. Gwendolyn Brooks, whose work gave a new and original voice to Chicago writing from its first publication, has been a generous supporter of workshops and publishing enterprises that have helped establish younger black writers such as Haki Madhubuti (Don L. Lee), Sterling Plumpp, Carolyn Rodgers, and Angela Jackson. In the past few years Chicago has become a center of poetic activity; several regular poetry reading series have run simultaneously in the city with steady audiences.

Chicago's special role in recent American literature has been as a center for alternative publishing. Paul Carroll's magazine *Big Table*, a notable example, provided the first publication for some of the most important writers to emerge in the 1950s. Third World Press, the Swallow Press, and *TriQuarterly* have had similar functions. These efforts have succeeded here, out of the immediate center of things in New York, in giving some sway to new and often radical work.

There is a sinking feeling that comes with ending a survey like this one; it has to do with fears over what has been left out. The best thing would be to publish such a ramble with extra-large margins and an open invitation to the reader to fill in what has been passed over or, in the shorthand look at the present, left out. Perhaps a great long list of names would do. I began with an anecdote that was intended to indicate briefly the richness and importance of Chicago literature. It may be that openly confessing to omission at the end is the way, finally, to make the point.

## 23

## Uncollected Faulkner

"On the day the carriage would be due, from daylight on the negro boy would squat beside the hitched droop-eared mule, shivering over the smoldering fire in the December rain beside the road which came up from Mississippi, with wrapped in an oil cloth cape a bouquet the size of a yard broom, and perhaps a hundred yards further up the road Charles Gordon himself sitting his horse in the rain too beneath a bare tree, watching the boy and the road."

This sentence opens William Faulkner's story "A Return," one of the best and richest of the previously unpublished tales collected in this new volume *Uncollected Stories of William Faulkner* edited by Joseph Blotner. It is vintage Faulkner, first submitted for publication in 1930, revised and resubmitted in 1938. The scene offered here is not just vividly pictoral; it has, as well, that sense of incipient allegory that illuminates so much of Faulkner: man, boy, black, white, road, tree, weather, season, fire, bouquet, the ceremonial distance between slave and master—every feature seems set in place like an icon. And the sentence itself is unfolded like a parchment heirloom, with practiced deliberation, the deft accents of "droop-eared mule" and "yard broom" anchoring it in a profane, real world.

What is being presented here is Randolph Gordon's well-polished version of his mother's reminiscences of her own courtship in the winter of 1861. At the center of the story there is an uneasy relationship between Randolph Gordon, a successful banker of 69, and Gavin Blount, M.D., a descendant of one of Randolph's mother's failed suitors. Gordon, like a number of Faulkner's characters, is a custodian of the past; Blount is a disenfranchised worshiper, who demands that Gordon rehearse the old stories again and again and finally coaxes him into inviting his mother to the Nonconnah Guards Ball, a re-creation of the ball she attended with Charles Gordon in 1861. At 41, Blount is so obsessed with the past that he presents himself as one of the old woman's contending suitors.

"A Return" involves a number of Faulkner's persistent concerns, and it deserves to be read in the company of his best stories. Much of what finds first publication in this collection is less impressive. Some of it is juvenilia, sketches Faulkner wrote just after he left Oxford, Mississippi, for New Orleans. Other stories never quite seem to catch their stride. "A Dangerous Man" begins with a wonderfully slapstick street fight and has a suitably credulous young narrator, but it ends rather abruptly. What is interesting about "A Dangerous Man" is that with certain Faulknerian elements in play at the start, a richly comic development is expected, and anything else is disappointing.

Throughout the section of unpublished stories there are familiar Faulkner characters. "With Caution and Dispatch" gives an account of part of John Sartoris's life in the R.A.F. that is not treated in *Sartoris*, and Popeye, from *Sanctuary*, appears in "The Big Shot." More persistent, though, is a general feeling of familiarity with the people and their settings. Many of these characters are early versions of later figures in Faulkner's fiction. Gavin Blount, M.D., for example, has a lot in common with Gail Hightower in *Light in August*. Finally, though, what is most striking about reading through 200 pages of new Faulkner is the familiar idiom felt in the first sentence of "A Return," the rare and immensely pleasurable sense of an enveloping fiction.

Everywhere in Faulkner, even in discarded pieces, there is a sense that character, event, and scene extend into a larger world that the fiction will eventually sustain. Invention is at once the delight and limitation of most short fiction; the quick imposition of character, early conflict, and resolution all require inventive agility. The advantage of Faulkner's short fiction is that it is always at work on something already there. Each story, however self-sufficient, has a part in a larger, more thorough invention. The effect is felt even when the precise connection with other stories and novels is unknown or, in the case of many of these unpublished stories, undeveloped. In some measure it is due to the fact that Faulkner's characters so often are collaborators in the larger invention, like Randolph Gordon, telling stories, or like Gavin Blount, obsessively listening.

I have lingered over the section of unpublished stories because it is the most pleasurable portion of a book largely devoted to the needs of scholars and the completion of the Faulkner canon. The book's first section, nearly half its 700 pages, is given over to printing the magazine versions of stories that Faulkner subsequently revised for inclusion in several novels, principally *The Unvanquished, The Hamlet,* and *Go Down, Moses.* Since these stories all became essential parts of major books, the earlier versions given here invite—even insist upon—comparisons with their more familiar forms—worthy and honorable work, certainly, but at some distance from the simple delights of discoveries like "A Return."

Still, these early versions provide a view of Faulkner at work, and Joseph Blotner's generous and readable notes serve as a guide to the complex developments that many of these stories had. In many cases these versions show stories in their embryonic stages: elsewhere the demands of magazine publication seem to explain a particularly short version. Occasionally, we are given a sense of a much more crucial revision. The difference between the *Scribner's* magazine version of "Spotted Horses" and the story in *The Hamlet* is the most dramatic. Faulkner had reworked the story of the wild horse auction several times. In the magazine version, most of the features of the tale are in place, but the story is told by Ratliff, one of the townspeople, in a first-person dialect narration. For *The Hamlet* he wrote the story again in the third person. The result is a much longer and much better story; everything seems to work with balance and perfection. The initial sighting of the horses has its carnival flair because of the distance the narration acquired, as does Flem Snopes's success at selling horses nobody can use. With Ratliff as narrator, "Spotted Horses" was very much a yarn, a familiar sort of front-porch or fire-house story. In the third-person version, something of the yarn remains, but the story acquires a larger comic dimension. The chaos that Flem and his horses visited on Frenchmen's Bend was a chaos the town somehow needed, a disorder in which, finally, even the court and justice participate. In its vitality, humor, and essential disarray, "Spotted Horses" is one of the best of Faulkner's stories, and it is useful to see, as we do here, how its final form resulted from what was initially a technical revision.

Included in this section also is the *Saturday Evening Post* version of "The Bear," a suggestive hunting story of just 15 pages, from which Faulkner evolved his most ambitious tale. Oddly, the short version has its own charm, perhaps because "The Bear" in its final metamorphosis has been weighed down with such a load of criticism and general metaphysical yearning by its most serious readers. The short story gives a little respite from the ponderousness the bear eventually acquired.

Often the differences between these stories in their magazine and book forms are far less pronounced, and reading through this section is encumbered by the need to fidget back and forth between texts. Though it would be less tidy, it is too bad that *Uncollected Stories* could not come to us in two separate volumes—one with the early versions of stories revised for book publication and another with the uncollected magazine stories of Blotner's second section and the final section of unpublished stories. The first would serve scholar and devotee; the second would extend the Faulkner available to more general readers. The problem is that a reader who takes up this volume, along with *The Collected Stories* and *Knight's Gambit*, will have a rather overcomplete collection of Faulkner stories skewed toward scholarship by the weight Blotner's *Uncollected Stories* gives to early versions.

## 24

## Stylish and Enthusiastic to the End:

## Cyril Connolly

The Introduction to Cyril Connolly's *The Evening Colonnade* is a fair introduction to Connolly himself. What we see is the aging man of letters gathering up a last decade's worth of book reviews and incidental essays in search of a quotation from which he might take his title. Like a bee returning to sample favorite flowers, he lights briefly on Lucretius, Horace, Dryden, Pope, Vaughan, Donne, Wordsworth, Pound, and Eliot, even testing a few exotic strains, Hafiz and Ramanujan, finally choosing a phrase from a rare romantic moment in Pope.

The excursion is delightful for the sense it offers of the passionate reader ensnared in his library—reading in one direction, then another, almost forgetting the chore that brought him there—and curiously reassuring. Book reviewing, Connolly's 30-year occupation, so easily produced literary Uriah Heaps—busy, short-sighted, scheming—that it is good to find the perennial reviewer for the *London Sunday Times* (and book editor of the *Observer*) at home with these poets. He was arcane, certainly, even precious, but so much better than the scout outings of our book-page Telemachi, stalking once a year the new *Ulysses* among a fresh crop of fat novels, turning back inevitably to their ledgers of reputation and prominence.

As a reader and a reviewer, Connolly was more a hedonist than a critic, and the self-conscious lyricism of his prose has about it that pornographic zeal you get from a gourmet talking you through some distant superb meal or from a discriminating traveler describing the morning air here or the nestled beach there.

Even his harsher judgments (his review of Mailer's *Presidential Papers*, for example, where he settles on the term "Caliban-Narcissus" for Mailer's brand of 20-century writing) have about them the resentment that comes when you suffer through an old favorite restaurant fallen on bad days, the personal disappointment and bitterness you can feel when you find a good view obscured by motels and billboards.

*The Evening Colonnade* has four sections. The first and most enjoyable is comprised of personal reminiscences and travel pieces; the second and third sections are made up of reviews of literary books, arranged chronologically into a section for traditional authors and a section for the moderns. The final section is a mixed bag, mostly reviews, that ranges from pieces on Max Ernst and Freud to a review of a book on shell collecting and a lovely model for what used to be called the *personal essay:* "Confessions of a House-Hunter."

The bits of personal history that open the first section are merely diverting. Connolly has done prep school (*The Condemned Playground*) and the 1920s better elsewhere. The short piece on Oxford is pleasant for the swath of famous names that wrapped Connolly's university days and that antique assurance with which they all *came down from Oxford*, like angels descending to a world somewhat deranged but still accommodating. I like best here the longer travel pieces. After giving two disappointingly short pieces on Venice (both of them reviews) and a mostly gastronomic "Farewell to Provence" ("A very creamy kind of scrambled egg with the local truffles chopped up in it." I said pornographic, didn't I?), Connolly settles in with four longish pieces on traveling in Africa. They are really the best the book has to offer; first, there's just more of Connolly, anxious over snakes and hyenas, memorizing survival tactics for dealing with the aggressions of hippos, rhinos, water buffalo, and elephants, exuberant over the evening air and the paradisal flowers. These descriptions offer his prose its widest reach. His natural descriptions are detailed and elegant, all the better for the sense you have occasionally that a scene is so amazing that even Connolly's feel for the right word won't manage it.

I must confess, though, that the African travel pieces annoyed me at first—too much concerned with lunches, dinners, and hotels, too many introductions to new friends. I resented the charming Cambridge-educated game wardens and parks commissioners who ambled in so often, blocking the African view, and was impatient with Connolly for denying me his excited descriptive prose.

But Connolly's sociability grew on me. The meetings, conversations, and carefully relished hotel dining rooms ultimately touch more of these African countries than the dazzle of the national parks. Recurrent here is the concern over the parks themselves and the wildlife, which are everywhere threatened by other pressing economic needs. Connolly becomes an apostle for African tourism—within the countries themselves the only economic justification for massive land preserves. Then, too, Connolly is an extremely fortunate pilgrim; he meets the heads of the parks, travels with authorities on birds and animals, and stops to chat with Pat Hemingway, Hugo Van Lawick, and Richard Leaky.

Out among the frangipani, on Lake George, listening to the hippos and describing the varieties of waterbirds, or as the jittery passenger in a small bush plane, Connolly is the best one can imagine. Even his jitters are stylish; an anxious night of strange animal sounds in a back country rest house is all the more solid for its anxiety, and the final trip in this series, to Senegal, is most vivid for being a general fiasco.

Connolly's criticism is best read for its enthusiasm and its stylishness, a kind of bibliomaniacal fun that is grounded in a range of serious reading as dazzling as any of his landscapes. He was no theorist and wrote best about books that rested most easily in his hands. It doesn't help that all these pieces are so short, two to four pages, or that they are primarily reviews of books generally about major writers and not direct treatments of major work. This was Connolly's native form, and he makes his way, finding in it a license for epigrammatic evaluation that might not be as acceptable else-where. The two literary sections of the book are composed chiefly of views of long-held passions and old friends through the critical and biographical dust that now trails (sometimes too thickly) behind them: Swift through Nigel Dennis; Pope through Peter Quennell and Aubrey Williams; James through Leon Edel; Hem-ingway through Carlos Baker; Pound through Noel Stock and Julian Cornell; Joyce through Richard Ellman.

This is almost inevitably not premier Connolly but rather the earnest nostalgia of an aging reviewer, redeemed constantly by an enviable sharpness of style and an unfailing ability to get back, however briefly, to what is best in the original works. I recommend most Connolly on Swift, Pope, Proust, and Symons. Among the moderns, there are fine pieces on Pound, especially on Pound's treason, Hemingway, Gide, Fitzgerald, and Auden, and I was delighted to find his review of Basil Bunting's *Briggflats* so generous in its praise.

Altogether *The Evening Colonnade* isn't a bad valedictory for Connolly. It isn't his best work, certainly, but it shows his range and occasionally gives us another view of his prose at its best, still eager, self-effacing, and observant.

In the mid-1940s one of his friends asked Wallace Stevens for a list of current books, good reading he might pass on to still another friend. Stevens's reply recommends a preface to logic, a book on aesthetics, and Cyril Connolly's *The Unquiet Grave* (1945), probably Connolly's best book. Stevens was the sort of man who took great care over gifts and suggestions to his friends and, in turn, responded with eloquent pleasure over gifts received. *The Evening Colonnade* deserves the same kind of deliberate, if not cautious, recommendation.

Give it to someone (yourself?) whose convalescence would be cheered by logic and aesthetics, who stays up nights with Elizabeth Bowen and reads *Country Life* magazine, remembers Ernest Dowson and Victor Plarr as more than footnotes to Pound's Mauberley; someone, that is, who could be taken with the ins and outs of shell collecting and relish a cocktail hour with the last few professional hunters in East Africa. Choose well. It's a rare treat, one of the last of its kind.

## 25

# A Quiet Master:

# V.S. Pritchett

The short story has been put on the critical list, pronounced dead, and laid to rest any number of times in the past few decades. Some of this distressing news was created by the general enthusiasm for apocalypse that infected criticism for the same period; much of it was the result of a shrinking market for short stories in major magazines and the suggestion by publishers that only poetry is harder to sell than collections of short fiction. Despite all of this, writers continue to be drawn to the form, and some readers, at least, remain loyal. The best guarantee that the form will survive lies in the fact that its pleasures are so uniquely its own. There is a memorability in stories that rarely exists in novels, a persistence not merely of character and scene but of language as well in the way that stories turn so completely on a single word or on a nuance of tone.

The best short-story writers give us some of the pure, personal touch of poets. The grand masters can seem at times to brood over the form like the great chess masters over ordinary games— Chekhov for emotional surprise, de Maupassant for irony, Joyce for precision, Saki for nuance, Hemingway for concision, Faulkner for poetic range, and lately, Barthelme for pure musical audacity. Some writers seem to take textures entirely to themselves—the rough, crosscut feel of Algren and Farrell, Fitzgerald's luster, the foxedlinen papers of Borges's imaginary library, Irvin Faust's uniquely American molded plastic. It is a form, like painting, of style by surface or color, that bows at times to landscape and portraiture.

V.S. Pritchett is one of the masters of the form, and his brief preface to this volume of *Collected Stories* offers the best description I know of the writer's interest in the short story. "I love the intricacies of the short form," he says, "the speed with which it can change from scene to scene. I have always thought that the writer of short stories is a mixture of reporter, aphoristic wit, moralist and poet—though not 'poetical'; he is something of a ballad-maker, and in the intricacy of his design close to the writer of sonnets. He has to catch our attention at once, to get the opening line right. He has to be something of an architect." The sense of complexity that Pritchett stresses here is true to the design of his stories but is not generally apparent in their surfaces. Pritchett's stories are disarmingly simple in language and narration. For some writers the world of the story is a conscious act of style, as though no leaf could stir but for the breath of its appropriate adjective. Pritchett takes an almost opposite course; his is a world of continuous, external implication. His characters arrive at their understandings in a welter of impinging detail, often unable to sort fully through their discoveries for themselves. Epiphanies come crowded among the ordinary crush of things, sometimes at the end of a dizzying string of reversals of attitude and feeling.

"When My Girl Comes Home," one of the longer pieces in the collection, is a fine example of Pritchett's technique and is his avowed favorite. The story opens at the reunion of a family with one of their members, Hilda Johnson, who has just returned from a post-World War Two imprisonment in Japan. Years before, Hilda had left London with her husband, an East Indian doctor, for a life in Singapore. The assumption has been that Hilda was captured and tortured by the Japanese, and that's the story that was covered by the newspapers. The reunion is brilliantly presented—a clamor of sentiment, good wishes, family bickering, and universal misunderstanding. Hilda, the family discovers by slow turns, was not imprisoned by the Japanese, but was married to a Japanese supply officer and so treated as a Japanese citizen. Her detainment was at the hands of the allies after the war. Pritchett's narrator is one of the younger members of this extended family, the brother of one of Hilda's first loves. Like most of Pritchett's first-person narrators, he tells the story out of the swirl of its events, caught in the same confusions as the rest of the family, with an investment in Hilda's legend that grew through the war with theirs and with his own discreet emotional investment as well, a kind of half-subdued romanticism inherited in part from his dead brother.

Hilda's return causes an upheaval in the whole family, but it is an upheaval of certainty, a test of the sustaining beliefs of the war and their anticipations for its conclusion. Each has years of conviction to reconstruct in the face of Hilda's great mound of luggage and American nylons, her bright, fashionable wardrobe, and her announcement that she'll soon be off to France to collaborate with a rich American on her life story, soon to be a major motion picture. "When My Girl Comes Home" is a study of disarray so exquisitely crafted that we are forced through the same strange turns the family takes. Early in the story, Harry Fraser, the narrator, sees Hilda as a woman without history, later as someone with "a life." Both observations are true and essential. Her absence from the "worm-eaten" history of their lives makes her the perfect test for each of them, and her possession of "a life" keeps her out of reach, even when she settles into an office job at a local factory. Hilda is a negative field against which everything else is seen anew, and Pritchett keeps her somewhat muddled and ordinary throughout, a Siren only by accident.

Hilda's counterpart in "The Saint" is Mr. Timberlake, a visiting evangelist from the Church of the Last Purification of Toronto, Ontario. In this story the narrator is a 17-year-old fundamentalist, a member of a sect that believes it is Error, evil, to accept the evidence of the sense over absolute faith in benevolent divine providence. Although he has withstood the jeerings of classmates and teachers, the narrator is afflicted with the beginnings of doubt and a growing attachment to the world of the senses. Mr. Timberlake's visit seems, at first, to free him from Error, but in the end merely confirms him in it. In the boy's imagination Timberlake is canonized at the same moment in which faith finally fails him. In a dazzlingly comic scene, Timberlake goes boating on the river with the boy and insists on taking the pole and teaching him to punt. The evangelist, despite the boy's warnings, ends up caught in the air on a willow branch and slowly descends into the river as the branch bends with his weight. It is Timberlake's refusal to acknowledge what has occurred that makes him a saint of the Last Purification and the boy's unshakable awareness of it that confirms all his doubts. Timberlake's suspension in the air is one of the perfected moments of Pritchett's skill as a short-story writer; it is wonderfully burlesque, of course, but it also carries the weight of the story, especially in the casual disregard that Timberlake's plight gets from the other punters who slip by as he descends, not because they are avoiding Error but merely because they are self-absorbed.

Both "The Saint" and "When My Girl Comes Home" depend entirely on Pritchett's skill in using first-person narrators. The same is true for many of his best stories—"The Camberwell Beauty," "The Fig Tree," and "The Diver," for example. No one I can think of uses first-person narrators with more skill and to such diverse effect. In "When My Girl Comes Home," much of the story's essential swirl of character rests on the familiarity with which Harry Fraser presents the gathered relatives. We believe in them even before they are quite distinguished from one another, in the same way that we credit the reality of the aunts and uncles of any intimately told anecdote of family life: They take life from a conviction of tone that can work only by never for an instant faltering. Pritchett carefully measures out the perceptiveness and the stylistic range of these narrators. In part this caution saves the charm of the narration, keeps it genuine and conversational and in character; it also provides Pritchett with an essential reserve in which a character "discovers" a style to meet a story's most important moment. At the conclusion of "The Camberwell Beauty," the failed lover sees the object of his desire in a new way and finds a new style in which to describe her.

Few of Pritchett's characters leap out of the text, ready to be transposed into other hypothetical situations. In fact, they tend to recede back into their stories, creatures of context. The odd agents of change and personal doubt—Hilda, Timberlake, Mrs. Pliny in "Camberwell"—are defined by the desires and anxieties of the people around them. Central characters rarely can survive as types; they are too much caught in the process of awareness. What is memorable is the way that these stories absorb us so quickly, drawing us into a world of small but intensely realized action, somehow convincingly contiguous with our own.

By contemporary standards of experimentation, Pritchett is a conventional fiction writer. He shares a commitment to detail and a sense of fiction's solid ground in the world with Balzac and George Meredith. Still, in a quiet way, he has expanded the range of the short story, both in his use of narration and in his ability to draw into the form a range of character and experience that we have come to expect only from extended novels of life and manners.

# VI

PART SIX

## 26

## Domestic Laughter:

## Liebling at Home

A. J. Liebling is one of several American journalists whose names are mentioned whenever writers discuss the great days of newspapers and magazines. Liebling, who lived until 1963, was a reporter for most of the New York papers and did several turns as a foreign correspondent. It was as a regular contributor to *The New Yorker*, though, that he was able to develop his own style, a wild mixture of big-city saloon savvy and literate urbanity. Stylistically the concoction is extremely rewarding. Liebling was at home with horse players and barkeeps but never far from a literary aside out of Stendhal or Shakespeare. His language is doubly barbed with the intricate business slang of bookies and bookish archaisms. He loves, almost to the point of distraction, paragraphs with odd turns in them or looping shifts of subject. This is not newspaper stuff generally, though Liebling's place is firmly set in the newspaper journalists' pantheon. Perhaps newspapermen love best the escapists from their ranks.

As personal and idiosyncratic as Liebling's style is in the five books reprinted here in *Liebling at Home*, there is very little of what we would call personality. In fact, it's difficult to find Liebling here at all, except as a negative figure described by the characters we see around him. This is not personal journalism. What we have instead is a shifting stance, suited to one of the boxers he portrays, a nonintellectual intellectual, an easily absorbed cynic, a curiously naïve savant.

There are a number of Lieblings here, and the most engaging is Liebling the master of the short, unexpected character study. No one is any better at catching the odd figures at the edge of society. Bouncers, hatcheck entrepreneurs, nickel-and-dime land swindlers, freak-show moguls, fight managers, bandless bandleaders, the thousand virtuosi of pawned instruments, sparring partners, club fighters, peddlers of genuine stolen neckties, and peddlers of phony stolen neckties—all were a part of Liebling's world: hustlers, mostly failed hustlers, who do their business in phone booths in Manhattan office buildings or in the shared offices of Liebling's fictitious Jollity Building. They are generally categorized as "telephone booth Indians," "nomads who have not yet attained that stage of pastoral culture in which they carry their own shelter." Instead, like hermit crabs they have to find a home abandoned by some other creature— the telephone booth. Of the five books collected here, *The Telephone Booth Indian* and *The Jollity Building*, which share the same midtown-Manhattan location and a cast of characters, are the most entertaining.

In general, telephone booth Indians are hopeful failures, conniving to use Bell's instrument without ever spending the nickels usually required. Some few manage a shared desk in the Jollity Building's communal offices. They hustle music, dancing girls, sight-seeing tours, even racing cockroaches—anything to avoid the painful alternative, ordinary labor. But Liebling added a few raging successes to the collection, as exemplars, perhaps, of the telephone booth Indian's quest. So we have profiles of Timothy J. Mara, one of New York's most successful bookies and the first owner of the New York Football Giants; the Shubert brothers, of Shubert Alley fame, who owned the lion's share of America's legitimate theatres in their day; and finally, Roy Howard, publisher of the

Scripps-Howard newspapers, who, Liebling said, dressed like a telephone booth Indian, which seemed enough to warrant his inclusion in this strange company.

Liebling liked, obviously, the boundless faith this tribe had in trickery and their tenacious eccentricity. At heart every hustler is an unacknowledged kingpin, a Barnum or a Shubert, but Liebling was interested, as well, in how their hustles worked. There is a wonderful range of information here about the care and pinchpenny feeding of boxers, the profit margin in hatcheck stands, odds-making, and exotic dancers. The most memorable of these hustlers are the devoted generalists like Count de Pennies, whose businesses included managing acquitted murderesses and gunmen's widows, Eskimos, mineral water, the aforementioned cockroaches, and lady boxers. The Count is the best of the Jollity Building's inopportun-ists, with a talent for undoing even the most likely of his swindles, the Dixie Melody Tours, for example, which turned an honest dollar until the count decided to pay the cooperating railroad with a bad check—in the words of the Jollity Building's manager, he was "a champion heel."

This is the same world that Damon Runyon treated with such success, but there is an important difference. Runyon specialized in broad comic strokes, depending for his style on the Broadway argot of his characters. Liebling was a stylish realist, and his flair for minor characters made him in some part an heir to Dickens and to Smollett. He had their eye for haberdashery and mannerism as the outward signs of character, as well as a fine ear for the intricate self-justifications of the habitual loser. We leave the Jollity Building convinced of its gritty reality and, like the author, at least half suspicious that there is very little to separate its hustle from legitimate business but success.

The most provocative of the books collected here is *Chicago: The Second City*. Liebling had nothing good to say about Chicago, but he said it at some length and very well. "It's like a curdled New York," he wrote, and these *New Yorker* pieces produced a flood of angry letters from irate Chicagoans. The letters, at least the most embarrassing of them, were included in the notes to the book when it was first published and survive in this edition, comic bits of huff-and-puffery that further condemn the city whose reputation they set out to save. In general, Liebling disliked Chicago's effrontery, its "World's Greatest Newspaper" brand of boosterism that thinly disguised an epidemic of self-contempt, but he also managed to dislike the city's skyline, the Loop, Ashland Avenue, Lake Michigan, the city's saloons and restaurants, its newspapers, the University of Chicago, Kup, and Sportsman's Park. As the deluging letter writers pointed out in 1952, this is all terribly unfair but, in the way of stylish nastiness, wonderfully amusing. If it bothers you, remember that it was all written more than 30 years ago, long before we became as beautiful and urbane as we are now. Imagine the hapless New Yorker stranded for two short visits and one extended stay in a city without Crate & Barrel or Rizzoli, before the *Tribune* stopped calling itself the Greatest in every edition or ironed the flag that it wears like a chip on the shoulder of its front page.

Clearly, what was wrong with Liebling's Second City was that it had none of the saving detail of his New York. There's no Jollity Building in Liebling's Chicago; so there's none of the delicious description or the extravagant unravelings of misdeeds. What remains is judgment, relieved only briefly by two portraits—one of Paddy Bauler, a character equal to any of his New Yorkers, and the other of Colonel McCormick. Both are marvelous, but I would recommend the book for its vitriol alone; it's so carefully prepared and lovingly decanted.

There are two book-length portraits collected here—*The Honest Rainmaker: The Life and Times of Colonel John R. Stingo*, the ambling biography of a horse tipster and journalist drinking friend of Liebling's whose real name was James A. Macdonald, and *The Earl of Louisiana*, a surprisingly warm and sympathetic treatment of Governor Earl Long. *The Honest Rainmaker* lost my interest eventually, though it begins with a wonderful series of misdirections that keep the story of the rainmaker in the title from being told. Macdonald is like the Jollity Building characters, an odds-on hustler and a fascinating one, but it is hard when following his adventures not to long for the variety and quick humor of the shorter portraits from the earlier book. Liebling's portrait of Long takes on some of the characteristics of his foreign reporting. Louisiana, unlike Chicago, was enough like a distant land to require some study. What emerges is a wonderful profile of the "mad" governor and a wonderfully detailed view of the politics out of which his madness grew.

*Liebling at Home*, the companion to last year's *Liebling Abroad*, is the kind of book to have around, something to dip into now and again. It's full of sharply focused observation, unexpected sympathy, and unwarranted judgment, grisly in an almost unfailingly pleasant way. Even its mistreatment of Chicago is finally charming and, in its own nagging way, flattering.

27

## In Chaos Sublunary:

## Ogden Nash

Most of the more popular and endearing definitions of poetry have to do with a poem's affect on the reader. Poems should make the hair on the back of your neck bristle, make your toes curl up or your eye-balls itch—all of which has to do with poetry's ability to move, disconcert, and even derange. Such bristlings, curlings, and itchings seem most appropriate to poems of vision or rhapsody, to natural beauty, passion, and the dark nights of the soul. They are less well suited to the wit, humor, word play, buffoonery, and inspired silliness of the poetry of Ogden Nash.

Still, in his own way Nash is disconcerting, sometimes maddeningly so. After even the briefest tour of this selected volume, you begin to think in farcical rhymes, clumping long, gangling sentences into unlikely couplets. The result is linguistic insouciance, which is more than a passing *nouciance*. Forgive me! The point is that it's hard to be serious or capture a tone that's imperious when rhyming has made you delirious. Oh, well. What makes Nash so infectious is not that he offers a stirring or desperate vision that you cannot help but share but that his quirkiness is so inescapable that he pretzels your language with his own. That's no small trick. In a number of poems Nash discusses the importance of humor (humorously, of course) and a comical view of things ("In chaos sublunary/What remains constant but buffoonery?"), and for the time you are hooked on Nash's jostling language, you are caught, as well, by his point of view. In 1930 Ogden Nash was working as an advertising copywriter for a publisher on Madison Avenue. At 28 he had already failed as a prep school teacher, a bonds salesman, and a sonneteer. As Archibald MacLeish's introduction has it, "Spring Comes to Murray Hill," written at his copywriter's desk, was the first poem Nash did in his characteristic style. MacLeish describes the invention not as verse but as rhymed prose. That first poem was published in *The New Yorker*, and Nash's first volume appeared the following year. In the next 40 years he published 20 books of poetry, 16 books for children, and several anthologies. The work was immensely successful. It's not very easy to say why.

The most familiar of Nash poems was short ("Candy/Is dandy-/But liquor/Is quicker"), but he more often wrote in longer sentence-lines, full of bizarre words and strange allusions. Nash is not really middlebrow, as you would expect from the size his audience or the easy television panelist disguise he found in the 1950s. What his form does is play various levels in among and against each other. Like Thurber, he had a lively sense of the fearsome character of ordinary life. "Life is stepping down a step or sitting in a chair/And it isn't there." For Nash these clumsy moments finally mark us all as companions of Shelley, who was once described "as a beautiful and ineffective angel beating his luminous wings against the void in vain/Which is certainly describing with might and main,/But probably means that we are all brothers under our pelts,/And Shelley went around pulling doors marked PUSH and pushing doors marked PULL just like everybody else."

MacLeish sees Nash as an essentially urban poet, someone who saw the city as a snarl of banalities. In this regard he compares Nash to Eliot, and as extreme as that sounds, there's more than a little justice to it. In that Shelley poem, which goes by quickly, hurrying to its pratfall final rhyme, there is a wonderful equation of that anonymous critic's "void" and city doors marked PUSH and PULL. Here's a short poem that could also serve MacLeish's comparison, called "The City:"

> Here men walk alone
> For most of their lives,
> What with hydrants for dogs,
> And windows for wives.

That's Eliot territory, all right, and it's easy to imagine Prufrock just down the block more seriously noticing "lonely men in shirtsleeves leaning out of windows." The point is that Nash, despite the foolery, maybe even because of it, was a modern, an observant and well-read one at that.

There are many surprises in these four hundred pages of Ogden Nash *I Wouldn't Have Missed It: Selected Poems of Ogden Nash.* One is his range. He wrote about everything—Mike Wallace's bad manners, television commercials, Henry Kissinger, parenthood, senility, Robert Burns, Freud, Aubrey's *Brief Lives*, martinis, and slipshod scholarship. His vocabulary was comical chiefly because of its size; it was immense. Swift said that good style consisted of proper words in proper places. Nash's style is made of odd words in odder places. For a poet known chiefly for the way he could twist and turn his language to a final joke, it is surprising how compact Nash could be and how much varied material he could get into a stanza. Here are two stanzas from "Exit, Pursued by a Bear" (the title's from Shakespeare's *A Winter Tale*):

> Pocks on the pink Picasso,
> Dust on the four Cezannes,
> Kit on the keys of the Steinway,
> Cat on the Louis Quinze—

*Rings on the Adam mantel*
*From a thousand bygone thirsts,*
*Mold on the Henry Millers*
*And the Ronald Firbank firsts*

an uncharacteristically harsh poem that ends with a reference to nuclear war. Still, there's a sharp side often to the more familiar Nashian themes—"To My Valentine," for example:

*More than the catbird hates the cat,*
*Or a criminal hates a clue,*
*Or the Axis hates the United States,*
*That's how much I love you.*

It's no surprise, though, that all of this is best taken in small doses. *I Wouldn't Have Missed It* is the sort of book that's good to have around, something to swig at at the end of a bad day—not wine or brandy, more like green Chartreuse or Creme de Violet, both quick and dandy, a pleasant and infectious medicinal. He belongs on the shelf with Ambrose Bierce and Josh Billings, perhaps nestling between the two of them, a more gentle misanthrope than Bierce and a more slyly vernacular comedian than Billings or the other local-color American humorists of the 19th century, with more to say about our daily predicaments than either one.

*I sit in the dusk. I am all alone.*
*Enter a child and an ice cream cone. . . .*

*Exit child with remains of cone,*
*Is it in the dusk, I am all alone,*

*Muttering spells like an angry Druid,*
*Alone in the dusk, with the cleaning fluid.*

28

## Old Obsessions, New Morals, Borrowed Prose:

## Spiro Agnew as Novelist

There was a time, as Spiro Agnew himself might have said with gusto a few years back, when being caught in the *act* (any one of several acts, really) meant that you would go hide, change your name, take up a lowly and anonymous profession, and never show your face in public again. Those were the good old days politicians like Agnew invariably praised—days of rustication, ostracism, scarlet letters, and the thief's brand, days of pride and mortification, halcyon days for moral fiber. Well, all that has fallen by the way. Nowadays, fame is a stepping stone to infamy, and infamy is the reason for writing a book.

Watergate, that nicest of all summer vacations, produced a good deal of moralizing, a scattering of brief fame, and an abundance of infamy, and in the new order of things, it has produced a huge number of books—books first from indictees, then from the wives of indictees.

Agnew's fall from the vice presidency, though not directly connected to Watergate, was a part of the same period, and we now have this book, *The Canfield Decision*, by Spiro T. Agnew, a novel about a Vice President. At its best it is just a middling political thriller that borrows from people like Allen Drury and Fletcher

Knebel, intent, that is, on showing the parries, feints, and lunges of political life, the intricate sword-play of that Zenda-on-the-Potomac from which America is governed.

Most of *The Canfield Decision* is given over to such fencing. We see the unfolding stratagems of V.P. Porter Canfield, the President's counterattacks, the pot-shots and positionings of some cabinet members and congressmen, and the constant hostilities of the media banditos. There are plots, conspiracies, and an Ian Fleming international intrigue.

This is all set in 1983. America has a lame-duck President who has run an even, steady government for nearly two terms, heavy on *detente* with the statesman-like Russian premier. Porter Canfield, the V.P. and protagonist, is intent on the presidency. His line of attack is similar to Kennedy's 1960 campaign, a mixture of social liberalism and alarmism over America's failing strength abroad. He breaks with the President over nuclear missiles for Israel. He wants them but wants more the conspicuous position the demand gives him in the media.

The elaborate plot of the novel involves Canfield's decision over Israel with the Iranian anti-communist movement, militant American Zionists, and finally the Chinese. In the course of all this Canfield's luster wears away, and in the end he is willing to accept any criminality in his own behalf.

Agnew's hero is young, handsome, and athletic, the sort of politician television commentators call charismatic. He is a Philadelphia lawyer, educated at Princeton and the Virginia Law School, with an immensely wealthy, socially prominent family. "He had," the book says, "the best of everything from the start." Canfield's undoing through the course of the novel is, then, the unmasking of the pretty, young, privileged liberal. Under the façade is the infinitely corrupting desire for power.

The fate that undoes Canfield, though, is not political but sexual.

This is also a novel of sexual desire. Except for passing glances at leggy secretaries by the sodden press corps, every desire by a male principal in the book is wonderfully requited—Canfield and the beautiful and mature Secretary of HEW, the chief of security and the beautiful and young private secretary, the resident egghead and the beautiful and sultry Iranian agent. These pairs all achieve an instant sunburst bliss, the sort of love for which Technicolor and the discreet fade-out were invented. "Suppose we're awful in bed together?" says the woman from HEW. "We won't be," replies the Vice President. It's nice to know rank still has some privileges.

In interviews Agnew has been distressed at the suggestion that the novel was ghosted for him, insisting that every word is his own, and the publicity material that came with my copy talks about writing it out by hand in hotel rooms around the world with pencils on yellow legal pads (those omnipresent yellow pads that gave Woodward and Bernstein a *leitmotif*). My sense is that Agnew had a lot of "help" with those pencil scribblings, not because the book is well written—it isn't—but because I can't imagine anyone so spontaneously burdened with so many cliched fictional devices. Such things are the rewards of years of tiresome diligence. Stylistically, this is a perfectly ordinary popular novel. It is not especially revealing about the vice presidency and adds nothing particularly new to our sense of political behavior.

Some of Agnew's old obsessions remain. His treatment of reporters is bitter, and he invents an organized conspiracy among newspaper, magazine, and television executives complete with code name, regular meetings, and policy decisions about manipulation of public opinion.

Overall, this is thin stuff. What is really interesting about this novel is that it's a novel. There is something more to this than Agnew's statement in the publicity that he couldn't write his memoirs while court cases were still pending. As true as that may be, I am also interested in the statement that he wrote the novel to regain his self-respect.

What Agnew is after here, I suspect, is the over-arching perception and understanding of the third-person narrator. Inside the mind of every contrivance, managing his main characters' unravelling of the complex assaults they perpetually suffer, conducting the book's final moral sorting out—those are redemptions that really count, for what they salvage is sensibility, and that must be no small matter to a man grown pasteboard in his highest moments, whose sudden fall was somehow off-hand and comic.

If Spiro Agnew is to become the hero of his own life—that promised or threatened book of memoirs—this gesture at control, this fiction, is understandably important to him. For the rest of us, the prospects for the future are frightening. John Dean and company have written confessions. On the higher rungs of the fallen ladder, Agnew and Ehrlichmann write novels. If the escalation continues, what we can expect to get from Nixon himself is an epic poem.

## 29

## Mike Royko's Rules for Living

There's a saloon I know on the South Side of Chicago, a no-name, street-corner place without a neon sign or a beer company's lighted plastic emblem to wag in the wind. It has a short, tilting bar that was obviously built to fit somewhere else, a few dinette tables, and a scattering of unmatched chairs that look as if they were retrieved from parking places after the last great snowstorm. There's a pool table done over in Mystik tape and just the suggestion of a back room created by a wall of beer cases. The owner, John, sits all night in an easy chair lifted above the concrete floor on pop-bottle crates, his stiffening legs propped up on an elevated hassock. Just behind his head is a framed portrait of Richard J. Daley, the one that was used on polling-place handouts, with cheeks that shine like the fenders on a Terra Plane.

For me John's place is bedrock Chicago, a genially scary sort of place where the regulars glower with world-class skill and hunch over their drinks with a seriousness that doesn't invite interruption. John's is not Royko territory. Of course they know his stuff; everybody does. And they like his indignation, his willingness to back the anonymous loser. It's a plight they all know pretty well. But they haven't forgiven him for needling the Mayor for all those years or for taking Bill Singer's part or the hippies' part, for throwing jabs at Parky Cullerton ("who never hurt nobody"), and for scratching at the 11th Ward. When it comes to their own territory, they quarrel with Royko. This is, after all, a neighborhood where "the Mayor" is a title that refers solely to Daley. Jane Byrne is called "the lady in City Hall," and Singer, for his long-silenced effrontery, is still known as "that little creep What's-his-name."

But, then, who else do they argue with? Not John Chancellor or Roger Mudd or Frank Reynolds. Television, for all its intimacy, is too remote for quarreling; it's too much a matter of cardigans and hairdos. The news simply washes over us all, like oil-covered water, leaving its own deepening stain. Royko's game is a close one, and even though his daily column in the *Sun-Times* is now syndicated in more than 200 papers, there is something tenaciously Chicago about all of his work. John's place may not be Royko territory; it's not Billy Goat's, nestled down under Michigan Avenue, where he spends a lot of time it seems, or one of the Northwest Side places his father once ran, but it is clearly a part of the Chicago he writes for and, in his own way, celebrates. There is, he keeps reminding us, an unreconstructed, undecorated, unchic Chicago full of regulars that has a flavor or rather a range of flavors worth keeping. Watch a good player at John's make an impossible shot by drifting the cue ball gently over the curled end of a piece of Mystik tape and you have a feel for it, the unaccountable skill that thrives among the gritty and thoroughly familiar.

*Sez Who? Sez Me* is a collection of recent Mike Royko columns, organized by subject. There is a section of tavern vignettes and a section on politics, plus chapters on bureaucracy, sports, contemporary lifestyles, and one called "The Birds and the Bees." What is amazing is how much of this survives as rereadable. Newspaper writing is not generally memorable; it's not supposed to be. Even columnists, freed of the grind of information, rarely manage much that you would want to come back to with interest. Royko's work persists, just as he does in the *Sun-Times* day after day, for a number of reasons. First, because he's a very good writer without ever really appearing to be one; that is, we never have the sense that he's struggling through his sentences like a fat man on a flight of stairs or that he's preening. Royko's style, which usually seems like no style at all, has its patented turns, of course. There is the flat, matter-of-fact narrative account of someone whose life has been manipulated by bureaucrats, in which absurdity is piled on absurdity with devilish care. He also has a fine comedian's sense of exaggeration, and no one is any better at lists, the passing catalogue with a comic twist in its tail. Arguing for his own expertise on the subject of drinking, for example, he lists the places where he's done "field research": "Chicago, Kansas City, Miami, San Francisco, Burlington, Wisconsin, New York, Washington, England, France, Germany, Cicero, and a few hundred other cities and countries."

Another source of the durability of so many of these columns is that there are several different Roykos. There is the chatty local character, rehearsing the quirks of the city and finding a curious but familiar pride in its harder edges. In one Billy Goat piece a rejected lover announces his intention to jump off a bridge over the Chicago River. "Don't do it," says an excursion-boat worker, tired of having corpses wash up against his pier. "Try the lake." At that point a smelt fisherman interrupts, saying that he and his friends are sick of having stiffs in their nets and that the young man should use the sewers. Another side of Royko is the muckraker. Still another is divertingly nostalgic, the fond memorialist of unspeakable Polish holiday dishes and the serial biographer of Slats Grobnik. His indignation at the gnawing injustices that officialdom perpetrates on the lone, unconnected individual makes him seem liberal, as does his selection of political targets, but there is a conservative strain there as well, in the distrust of the fashionable and an insistence on uncomplicated values. Lifestyles offend him for their escape from both life and style. The running craze is countered with a column on Long-Term Sitting, and the word "relationship" is imposed on the lyrics of a dozen love songs, beginning with "I'm in the mood for a relationship, simply because you're near me." Underlying this playfulness is a faith in our ability to see the absurdity of such things once they are exposed or lifted whole from their usual protective covering and set down in a more ordinary context.

What Royko is jousting at throughout this collection is the ease with which we put up with and even learn to accept the ridiculous and the truly horrible because they are layered over with high purpose ("significant other" instead of boyfriend or girlfriend) or governmental regulation. His column on the tenth anniversary of the 1968 Democratic National Convention is not a retracting of the events of August 1968 but an account of the arrest of a Vietnam veteran for riding his wheelchair down the streets of De Soto, Missouri, in July 1978. Against the squabbles and nostalgias of 1968, Royko poses a stark reality—Ralph Durain toppled from his wheelchair on the floor of a Missouri jail house, his untended prosthetic device infecting his bladder—a commemoration in fact of the business of 1968 and a reminder that callousness and stupidity are still with us.

*Sez Who? Sez Me* is varied. To say that it is also uneven does little more than acknowledge a daily column as its source. More frequently it is sharp, funny, satirical, and occasionally angry. The regulars at John's place would be consoled by rereading the tribute to the Mayor that appeared in the paper just after his death, in which Royko salutes Daley for being "pure Chicago." *Pure Chicago* is one of Royko's charges. He tends it with real care, something I imagine John and his Canaryville customers would acknowledge, and that's not bad for a North Sider, not bad at all.

## 30

## Taking Lake Shore Drive

It is called simply *the Drive*, singular and auspicious, something primary, given, part of the City's grand peerage—the Lake, the Loop, the River, the El, the Drive. "Take the Drive," they say. "Just go down this street till you hit the Drive, and you're home free."

Take it. The Drive. It's all yours. Alone behind the wheel, the radio playing . . . love's old sweet song or love's regret . . . the city shines like a half-remembered promise someone kept. This is how it was supposed to be, beautiful and bright, as dazzling as Oz or El Dorado, a home for your heart's desire. The play of water on the rocks, indolent sailboats, the subtle choreography of morning runners in their blue, expensive shoes, trees, grass, the drawbridge that pulses like a vein—all conspire to give the city a coherence it does not otherwise have. Even the occasional sight-gags along the way—the tin rocketship, Stephen Douglas hoisted like a sentinel above the South Side, a timber stockade, a submarine, a totem pole, the word "Kraft" in gold relief, like an annunciation—even these confirm the order, frolics for the eye or the half-attentive mind. Drive.

Take it easy—the stately concourse through Grant Park, the Field Museum's meticulous classicism at one end, Standard Oil's enormous Doric gas pump at the other. Nice and easy—past the costume jewelry geodesic dome that somehow makes the effrontery of Outer Drive East amusing, into the "S" curve, that proving ground for shock absorbers and lunatics. Sidle to the right, remembering always that the guy next to you can't drive, has four bald tires, and will cross two lanes making the second curve. You ease around him and glide down the hill past the shoal of turning signals at Ontario Street, the lake at your side now like a sleek companion. Suddenly, your nagging, self-centered car seems worth it after all, and you slip past the Gold Coast, the tight double curve where oiled bodies gather sand all summer and wealth seems so reasonable.

Free and easy—the long, narrow pastoral running north. Fullerton, Belmont, Wilson, wherever you like, you're home free. It is the surviving accomplishment of Daniel Burnham's great plan for the city of Chicago, a remnant of an age that believed in coherence, proportion, grand vistas and design enduring a world in which they seem unlikely, if not impossible. This isn't an expressway, one of those purgatorial basements built for frustration and semi-trailer trucks; it's a drive. The Drive. Take it.

31

# Re-Entry: Chicago

*"Now, as I said, the way to the Celestial
City lies just through this town where this
lusty fair is kept; and he that will go to the
city, and yet not go through this town, must
needs "go out of the world."*

Portland, Oregon. Cold November rain the whole weekend, all the
green and pleasant sublimity of the Northwest foreclosed. Toward
the airport the highway begins to ice over, and the water on the car
windows lingers in slowly descending baguettes. Along the way,
motels and massage parlors, their neon signs running like candle
wax—the free parking, fast service, color TV in all rooms, polyester
fray of every city in America, even more garish at night in the
rain—water on the streets and along the car's windows catches the
colors like tinsel or spins them into angel-hair circles around
streetlamps and headlights. McDonald's Golden Arches have an airy
thinness about them, and the florescent lights of the food service
area shine from their glass enclosure like the facets in a diamond
solitaire. The Earthly Pleasures Salon glows like a pinched cheek.
Suddenly, the airport, with its uniform blue signs and high ticket
counters. A quick farewell and a dash to the departure gate.

"Chicago. Smoking. Thank you."

Wet snow and no jetway in Spokane. Snowflakes in the landing lights, a moment of tension from *Airport* as we all descend the aluminum gangplank—they call it deplaning—and cross into the low terminal, drip awhile, then file out to a 707 waiting in the snow. Airborne, I chat with a woman from Pullman, dressed head to foot in Pendleton. In a dream over Montana she reveals herself to me as an Indian princess. The Pendleton, she says, is a disguise. Awake, I decide that she is the spirit of the Northwest, all woodsy heartiness, her bright eyes nestled in piney wrinkles. She sleeps the sleep of the just, the unfretted sleep so many Haight-Ashbury refugees have gone to Oregon and Washington to find, a sleep as green as a sunlit haze over the San Juans. The Princess says that she is a direct descendant of Sacajawea and that it is her task to guide me back from the mouth of the Columbia.

Minneapolis for an hour's layover. I de-plane into a great gallery of departure lounges. In the center are several rows of cushioned steel chairs with swing-away, coin operated television sets. It is 1:30 a.m., and a dozen or so passengers are scattered along the first row, each watching the same late show on his own screen. It's like the dogwatch at Mission Control. A hard rain beats against the dark glass that encloses the gallery. Outside, a rhinestone and sequined light swirls over the ground crews. On all the television screens Charleton Heston in buckskin shouts silently at Fred MacMurray.

The last time I flew from Minneapolis to Chicago was the Saturday after Martin Luther King's assassination. In the landing pattern to O'Hare we could see the west Side of the city burning, as though it had been bombed by a squadron of planes just ahead of ours. Tonight, the city has a chilly clarity. Streetlights pillow suburban streets. The expressways pump slowly. It's past four in the morning, and O'Hare is as quiet as it ever gets, empty enough to seem like some newfangled monument. The fixtures protrude, or rather, obtrude: light fixtures, suspended television screens flicking arrivals and departures, empty check-in counters, water fountains and fire hoses in bas-relief, red coin-operated newspaper vendors, a stand-up cocktail bar closed for the night. A gallery of unnoteworthy objects thrust into view—an exhibition, of sorts. I think of the Auditorium Theatre's celebration of the electric light bulb, Louis Sullivan's coherent faith in technology and its continuousness, the way the light bulbs are pearled along its heavy arches, a delicacy that diagrams its classic lines of stress. The airport's array of gadgets is mere accumulation against minimal surface. The junk is more substantial than the walls. It is the primary surface of O'Hare, monument to a surfeit of hardware. That's why all airports seem so much alike; the essential parts are interchangeable. Portland, Spokane, Minneapolis, Chicago—half a continent's worth of the great American airline terminal—terminal, now, in the contemporary sense, something you plug into.

The concourse ends in a maze of security gear, two clutters of leftover Holiday Inn parts and electronic debris. None of it seems particularly secure in itself—an appropriately awkward setting, I suppose, for seeing the insides of an overnight bag in X-ray, shadowgrams of shaving cream, razor, toothbrush, books, soiled underwear. The attendants have a boredom about them that must go with such godlike vision. I pass it all by. You don't have to be checked on the way out. I am leaving America's last Arcadia, that fractured pastoral made up of the departure concourses of hundreds of airports and their little jet-propelled canisters of sky—the fifty-first state, freed by metal detectors and high-speed gamma rays from guns, knives and cudgels, the ultimate suburb. Where else in America can you be so sure that the person sitting next to you is not carrying some kind of deadly weapon? Leaving this otherworld, as tinny and insubstantial as it is, you return home, quickly putting on all the protective paranoias that get you by day to day. The chumminess of your fellow skysailors begins to collapse almost immediately; by the time you reach the baggage carrousel, the jostling competition of buses and subways has returned. You also pass into a period of special vulnerability. You are markedly, now, someone without a weapon. However meek and mild you may be, it is otherwise possible for your thousands of potential attackers to think that you might be carrying a gun.

I heave my bag, then myself into the back seat of a taxi—no airport buses this time of night. The driver is a woman with a moon face and hair up in blond woodshaving curls. It's the Ford City Shopping Center up-do, just out of enormous plastic curlers and uncombed. She is heavy and fits rather too snugly under the steering wheel, so turns it with short gestures at the sides. We move out past the O'Hare Inn and onto the highway, flanked with still more inns, O'Hare's very own transient's paradise of restaurants, bars and show lounges. Businessmen now travel to Chicago and never enter the city itself, loitering here, instead, in an underbrush of doubleknits waiting for morning meetings in their hotels or out among the hundreds of regional offices that spread from the airport, drab low structures mostly that sport their corporate logos like boutonnieres. The driver asks where I've been. I answer. Am I in business? I tell her that I teach. High school? No, college. That's her cue.

"You know I read all that stuff once. I was really good at it, too. In high school, I was in college prep . . . read all that stuff, books and everything. Everybody said I should go to college."

Out the window the hotels and regional offices subside to the tidiness of the northwest side, an orderliness of red and green asphalt roofing above textured brick house fronts.

"Got married instead. And my husband? He was one of them guys don't want his wife to know nothin. He'd come home, find me readin a book and get mad as hell. He kept me down, know what

I mean? I mean he didn't want me readin or nothin. And what could I do? Cause I got pregnant right away. Three kids—damn good kids too—before I got my divorce. You know what I regret most?"

There's not really time to say, what?

"Not going to college, like everybody said I should. But you know when I was coming up, everything was marriage, everything! You went to a movie and it was all sweetness and light, you know what I mean? Everybody'd fall in love and get married and go off into the sunset. And the comics? They was just the same . . . love and marriage and sunsets. Boy, was I ever dumb. All of us, all of us was dumb. Go steady, get engaged, get married. That's what all of us did back then. This here *new morality?* Whatever you say about it, it's all right with me cause girls ain't so dumb."

She pauses, and I consider saying something about movie sunsets and the sexual revolution, then think better of it.

"Sweetness and light. What a laugh! You get married and you find out real quick. First time you see that thing of his you find out. Five years, three kids—that's how long it took me to get out. I only stayed that long cause I thought I was supposed to . . . just like my mother. She never had it no better. You think she'd tell me anything? No, just more sweetness and light. My oldest girl? She's goin' on sixteen, and I'll tell you, she wants to go to one of them X movies, I'll give her the money myself. Honest! Better to see it that way, better than all that Debbie Reynolds crap we used to go to. Sweetness and light. How dumb can you get?"

We are into the junction of the Kennedy and the Edens expressways. At the top of the rise you can see the Loop, skewed slightly because of the highway's odd angle so that the Hancock building and the Sears Tower seem quite close together. *Kennedy, Edens, the Loop, Hancock, Sears*—entering Chicago is like coming upon the shuffled remnants of an allegory you are supposed to understand and reassemble. My blond familiar is talking about her daytime job as a receptionist for a plumbing company. There's this guy, a real gentleman, who comes in every week for one of the suppliers (Why not Royal Quiet Flush, my all-time favorite?), and she's been seeing him. It sounds sylvan, almost like "keeping company." Then suddenly, she's back at her marriage, her husband's lack of respect for her and "that thing of his," which has become thematic to her monologue. Each time it enters one of her sentences something more is said. Like a composer, she's working by carefully plotted steps toward a full-fledged description.

"That thing . . . just like the church says, I came to my marriage pure . . . That thing . . . like the church says . . . I didn't have the slightest idea . . . Course I had brothers, but it ain't the same . . . That thing . . . like the church says . . . I always wanted kids." No doubt about it, if the ride lasts long enough, she'll describe her whole wedding night, but there are diversions, embellishments, perhaps—her plumbing supplies sales-man, a good restaurant on south Harlem Avenue, her kids, and for tympani, regular verbal assaults on the few other drivers on the highway. She returns to "that thing," then veers away. I forget the terrain, and quite abruptly, we're in my driveway. She hasn't done it yet. I say something about things working out for the best and hand her a twenty-dollar bill. She has no change, she says, and suggests we head over to Bridgeport to an all night gas station, one of those big discount places with milk by the plastic gallon and cut-glass premiums. But after 10:00 it's correct change only accord-ing to the sign over the pumps.

AFTER 10 PM.
ATTENDANT HAS NO MONEY
MONEY KEPT IN SAFE
ATTENDANT HAS NO KEY
EXACT CHANGE SALES ONLY!

I tell her to drive on to Halsted Street, and she begins her polyphonic confession once again. We reach Ed's Snacks—Breakfast Anytime, and I run in for change.

As I start back into the cab, someone screams at me from the middle of the intersection. Incredible, the corner is dark; David's across the street is closed; Ed's has only one customer, and suddenly, from the middle of the street there's a woman screaming at me. She's wearing glittered, three-inch platforms, a bright dacron dress and one of those Ginger Rogers fur jackets—tall and very thin, with a hairdo of frosted Dynel, running, or rather, spindling toward me. "That's my cab!" Close up, she looks like a Charles Addams version of a hooker; her mascara is smudged over her eyelids, and her face is extremely pale. The snags at the corners of her mouth are alcoholic, but her eyes are pure Dexadrine. I explain that it's *my* cab and tell her about stopping to get change. I even show her the change.

"Well, what the hell am I supposed to do. I'll never get another cab out here." Somehow, it's all my fault, and without knowing quite why, I accept the blame, finally agreeing to let her ride back home with me, then take the cab for herself. The driver is displeased by the whole thing but gives in. We start back, and the driver takes up her story, somewhat desperately now. At the same time, my fellow passenger decides that stopping for a while at my place would be better than keeping the cab.

"Well, I don't see why we couldn't have just one drink."

"Ain't none of my kids gonna be as dumb as I was, I can tell you that for sure."

". . . really, no hurry at all . . ."

". . . like the church says . . ."

". . . cause, I mean, you really helped me out of a jam back there . . ."

". . . that thing, the first time I saw it . . ."

". . . I didn't know what to do."
". . . I didn't know what to do."

At my door again, I pay the driver what is by now a ridiculous fare. The driver keeps talking as she takes the money; my new companion has her hand on my arm. In the light from the lobby I can see both their faces—one round, the other almost skeletal, both circled by outrageously unreal auras of hair. The one in back slouches into the seat, the matted fray of her wig scraping the textured vinyl loudly. The driver says, "What I'll always regret is that I didn't go to college like everybody said I should," and pulls herself under the steering wheel. They back out of the driveway together and drive off into the sunrise, somehow meant for each other.

## COLOPHON

The text was set in Bembo with running heads set in Line Block Gothic. Bembo is a type derived from the work of Aldus Manutius and Francesco Griffo in Venice in the late 15th and early 16th centuries. The original type was cut for the publication of Cardinal Bembo's *De Aetna* which served as the prototype for this face and the work of Claude Garamond.

This book was composed by Books International, Deatsville, Alabama. The book was printed by the Princeton University Press, Lawrenceville, New Jersey on acid free paper.